PRENTICE HALL
Algebra 1

Practice Workbook

Prentice
Hall

Needham, Massachusetts
Upper Saddle River, New Jersey
Glenview, Illinois

ISBN 0-13-044398-0

23 09 08

Contents

Contents

Arithmetic Review Worksheets

The following five blackline masters are arithmetic review worksheets. Each one provides additional exercises for fundamental arithmetic skills and concepts. They are keyed to the five parts of the Fundamental Skills Test found in the *Prentice Hall Algebra 1 Assessment* supplement.

You will find these worksheets helpful for students needing extra practice on decimals, fractions, percent, and the metric system.

Add.

1. $\begin{array}{r} 14.31 \\ +\ 3.61 \\ \hline \end{array}$

2. $\begin{array}{r} 3.008 \\ +\ 9.779 \\ \hline \end{array}$

3. $\begin{array}{r} 173.5 \\ +\ 5.28 \\ \hline \end{array}$

4. $\begin{array}{r} 54.93 \\ +\ 27.555 \\ \hline \end{array}$

5. $\begin{array}{r} 92.34 \\ 66.81 \\ +\ 37.98 \\ \hline \end{array}$

6. $\begin{array}{r} 129.1 \\ 88.36 \\ +\ 60.85 \\ \hline \end{array}$

7. $\begin{array}{r} 0.0095 \\ 0.0484 \\ +\ 0.0778 \\ \hline \end{array}$

8. $\begin{array}{r} 62.717 \\ 39.447 \\ +\ 86.225 \\ \hline \end{array}$

9. $33.12 + 4.99$

10. $1531.27 + 21.99$

Subtract.

11. $\begin{array}{r} 28.9 \\ -\ 19.7 \\ \hline \end{array}$

12. $\begin{array}{r} 47.84 \\ -\ 9.39 \\ \hline \end{array}$

13. $\begin{array}{r} 0.2 \\ -\ 0.145 \\ \hline \end{array}$

14. $\begin{array}{r} 14.53 \\ -\ 9.65 \\ \hline \end{array}$

15. $\begin{array}{r} 4.102 \\ -\ 0.003 \\ \hline \end{array}$

16. $\begin{array}{r} 100.01 \\ -\ 84.56 \\ \hline \end{array}$

17. $\begin{array}{r} 12.4 \\ -\ 9.55 \\ \hline \end{array}$

18. $\begin{array}{r} 0.1884 \\ -\ 0.0937 \\ \hline \end{array}$

19. $3.192 - 2.201$ _____

20. $21.57 - 20.48$ _____

Multiply.

21. $\begin{array}{r} 3.7 \\ \times\ 0.8 \\ \hline \end{array}$

22. $\begin{array}{r} 0.031 \\ \times\ 0.8 \\ \hline \end{array}$

23. $\begin{array}{r} 30.5 \\ \times\ 0.76 \\ \hline \end{array}$

24. $\begin{array}{r} 25.12 \\ \times\ 0.09 \\ \hline \end{array}$

25. $\begin{array}{r} 3.22 \\ \times\ 0.0007 \\ \hline \end{array}$

26. $\begin{array}{r} 1345.62 \\ \times\ 0.0301 \\ \hline \end{array}$

27. $\begin{array}{r} 5.17 \\ \times\ 0.48 \\ \hline \end{array}$

28. $\begin{array}{r} 0.87 \\ \times\ 3.5 \\ \hline \end{array}$

29. 7.506×0.28

30. 2.1101×3.1

Divide.

31. $6 \overline{)15.12}$ _____

32. $4 \overline{)7.28}$ _____

33. $9 \overline{)2.511}$ _____

34. $4.2 \div 15$ _____

35. $0.46 \div 50$ _____

36. $10.01 \div 7$ _____

Find the quotients to the nearest hundredth.

37. $5.8 \overline{)30.8}$ _____

38. $4.8 \overline{)6.75}$ _____

39. $0.72 \overline{)0.915}$ _____

40. $12.4 \div 0.9$ _____

41. $5.55 \div 0.15$ _____

ARITHMETIC REVIEW 2
Fractions—Basic Operations

NAME _____

DATE _____

Add or subtract.

1. $\dfrac{10}{12} - \dfrac{2}{3}$ _____

2. $\dfrac{11}{33} - \dfrac{5}{35}$ _____

3. $12\dfrac{3}{5} - 3\dfrac{1}{4}$ _____

4. $7\dfrac{1}{4} - 3\dfrac{3}{5}$ _____

5. $9\dfrac{3}{4} + 7\dfrac{5}{8} + 5\dfrac{3}{12}$ _____

6. $5\dfrac{1}{3} + 2\dfrac{1}{2} + 3\dfrac{3}{4}$ _____

7. $\dfrac{5}{30} + \dfrac{7}{21}$ _____

8. $\dfrac{7}{28} + \dfrac{12}{18}$ _____

9. $60\dfrac{2}{5} - 32\dfrac{4}{5}$ _____

10. $12\dfrac{7}{8} - 4\dfrac{3}{4}$ _____

11. $12\dfrac{1}{8} - 5\dfrac{1}{4}$ _____

12. $7\dfrac{3}{5} - 5\dfrac{4}{5}$ _____

13. $\dfrac{3}{8} - \dfrac{6}{24}$ _____

14. $\dfrac{14}{56} - \dfrac{3}{21}$ _____

15. $\dfrac{17}{5} - 2$ _____

16. $\dfrac{81}{4} - 6$ _____

17. $7 + \dfrac{32}{5}$ _____

18. $27 + \dfrac{15}{7}$ _____

19. $6\dfrac{1}{7} + 5\dfrac{2}{5}$ _____

20. $7\dfrac{3}{4} + 2\dfrac{1}{5}$ _____

21. $8\dfrac{7}{8} - \dfrac{25}{3}$ _____

Multiply or divide. Reduce all fractions.

22. $\dfrac{5}{3} \cdot \dfrac{11}{3}$ _____

23. $\dfrac{2}{5} \cdot \dfrac{7}{3}$ _____

24. $\dfrac{7}{11} \cdot \dfrac{44}{7}$ _____

25. $\dfrac{35}{6} \cdot \dfrac{33}{49}$ _____

26. $\left(2\dfrac{3}{5}\right) \cdot 3$ _____

27. $\left(1\dfrac{3}{5}\right) \cdot \left(\dfrac{10}{3}\right)$ _____

28. $\left(2\dfrac{3}{8}\right) \cdot \left(\dfrac{3}{5}\right)$ _____

29. $\left(5\dfrac{1}{7}\right) \cdot \left(2\dfrac{3}{4}\right)$ _____

30. $\left(3\dfrac{5}{8}\right) \cdot \left(2\dfrac{2}{5}\right)$ _____

31. $\left(\dfrac{55}{121}\right) \cdot \left(2\dfrac{17}{5}\right)$ _____

32. $\dfrac{5}{3} \div \dfrac{11}{3}$ _____

33. $\dfrac{2}{5} \div \dfrac{3}{7}$ _____

34. $\dfrac{7}{11} \div \dfrac{3}{11}$ _____

35. $\dfrac{15}{14} \div \dfrac{12}{35}$ _____

36. $\left(2\dfrac{2}{3}\right) \div \left(3\dfrac{1}{3}\right)$ _____

37. $\left(3\dfrac{1}{8}\right) \div \left(3\dfrac{4}{5}\right)$ _____

38. $\left(5\dfrac{2}{3}\right) \div 4$ _____

39. $3 \div \left(2\dfrac{1}{8}\right)$ _____

40. $\left(3\dfrac{3}{5}\right) \div \left(2\dfrac{1}{3}\right)$ _____

41. $\left(2\dfrac{3}{5}\right) \div \left(1\dfrac{1}{3}\right)$ _____

42. $\left(3\dfrac{3}{5}\right) \div \dfrac{2}{3}$ _____

43. $\dfrac{3}{8} \div \left(3\dfrac{8}{3}\right)$ _____

Find a prime factorization for each of the following.

1. 5460 _____ **2.** 2541 _____ **3.** 1071 _____ **4.** 1170 _____

Reduce.

5. $\dfrac{52}{36}$ _____ **6.** $\dfrac{27}{63}$ _____ **7.** $\dfrac{21}{24}$ _____ **8.** $\dfrac{42}{105}$ _____

9. $\dfrac{356}{124}$ _____ **10.** $\dfrac{264}{462}$ _____ **11.** $\dfrac{2730}{461}$ _____ **12.** $\dfrac{1012}{26565}$ _____

Rewrite as a mixed fraction. Reduce.

13. $\dfrac{25}{2}$ _____ **14.** $\dfrac{63}{27}$ _____ **15.** $\dfrac{54}{6}$ _____ **16.** $\dfrac{21}{5}$ _____

Rewrite as a fraction.

17. $3\dfrac{5}{8}$ _____ **18.** $2\dfrac{1}{7}$ _____ **19.** $15\dfrac{3}{11}$ _____ **20.** $12\dfrac{2}{3}$ _____

Find the reciprocals for each of the following.

21. $\dfrac{3}{4}$ _____ **22.** $\dfrac{12}{2}$ _____ **23.** 2 _____ **24.** $\dfrac{8}{5}$ _____

Find the LCM (least common multiple) for the following pairs.

25. 14, 35 _____ **26.** 105, 154 _____ **27.** 28, 42 _____ **28.** 24, 36 _____

Find the GCF (greatest common factor) for the following pairs.

29. 60, 64 _____ **30.** 105, 42 _____ **31.** 154, 28 _____ **32.** 60, 35 _____

Write each decimal as a mixed fraction. Reduce all fractions.

33. 0.04 _____ **34.** 3.28 _____ **35.** 7.64 _____ **36.** 30.14 _____

37. 0.0002 _____ **38.** 1.12 _____ **39.** 3.05 _____ **40.** 0.77 _____

41. 0.66 _____ **42.** 0.3 _____ **43.** 0.125 _____ **44.** 0.375 _____

Write each fraction as a decimal.

45. $\dfrac{9}{15}$ _____ **46.** $\dfrac{33}{50}$ _____ **47.** $5\dfrac{4}{5}$ _____ **48.** $\dfrac{327}{1000}$ _____

49. $\dfrac{7}{20}$ _____ **50.** $3\dfrac{5}{8}$ _____ **51.** $2\dfrac{3}{4}$ _____ **52.** $\dfrac{1}{3}$ _____

Convert each of the following as indicated.

1. 0.033 to percent _____

2. 3.11 to percent _____

3. 0.035% to decimal _____

4. 29.5% to decimal _____

5. $\frac{3}{5}$ to percent _____

6. $\frac{5}{4}$ to percent _____

7. 35% to a reduced fraction _____

8. 28% to a reduced fraction _____

Solve.

9. Find 22% of 350. _____

10. Find 135% of 400. _____

11. 5% of what is 240? _____

12. 120% of what is 350? _____

13. Find what percent of 40 is 12.5. _____

14. Find what percent of 25 is 40. _____

15. The number of entries in a race decreased 20% from 530 entries in last year's race. Find the new number of entries. _____

16. The number of accounts with a certain firm increases 30% from a level of 200 accounts. Find the new number of accounts. _____

17. The number of gas stations in a city increases from 120 to 150. Find the percent increase. _____

18. The amount of money in a savings account decreases from $340 to $220. Find the percent decrease rounded to the nearest tenth of a percent. _____

19. Acme Manufacturing's daily production of widgets is 140% of its competition's. If the competition produces 1230 units per day, how much does Acme produce? _____

20. Grace has 85% of the total points possible in her science class. If there are 350 points possible, how many points does Grace have? _____

LENGTH		MASS	
millimeter (mm)	= 0.001 meter	milligram (mg)	= 0.001 gram
centimeter (cm)	= 0.01 meter	centigram (cg)	= 0.01 gram
decimeter (dm)	= 0.1 meter	decigram (dg)	= 0.1 gram
meter (m)	= 1.0 meter	gram (g)	= 1.0 gram
dekameter (dam)	= 10 meters	dekagram (dag)	= 10 grams
hectometer (hm)	= 100 meters	hectogram (hg)	= 100 grams
kilometer (km)	= 1000 meters	kilogram (kg)	= 1000 grams

CAPACITY	
milliliter (mL)	= 0.001 Liter
centiliter (cL)	= 0.01 Liter
deciliter (dL)	= 0.1 Liter
liter (L)	= 1.0 Liter
dekaliter (daL)	= 10 Liters
hectoliter (hL)	= 100 Liters
kiloliter (kL)	= 1000 Liters

VOLUME

Volume has dimensions of length cubed. One cm^3 has the same volume as a cube that measures 1 cm on a side. One cm^3 has a capacity of 1 mL.

Complete.

1. 1 m = _____ mm

2. 1 cg = _____ g

3. 1 dL = _____ L

4. 1 dL = _____ daL

5. 1 hm = _____ dam

6. 1 kg = _____ cg

7. 300 g = _____ kg

8. 0.0002 kL = _____ L

9. 500,000 mm = _____ dam

10. 234 mL = _____ L

11. 0.994 m = _____ mm

12. 1.56 cm = _____ m

13. A room is 10 m by 10 m. Find the area of the room.

14. A picture is 10 cm by 10 cm. Find the area in m^2.

15. 100 cm^2 = _____ m^2

16. 1 m^2 = _____ cm^2

17. 1 m^3 = _____ cm^3

18. 1000 cm^3 = _____ m^3

19. 450,000 cm^3 = _____ m^3

20. 0.00005 m^3 = _____ cm^3

21. 354 mL = _____ cm^3

22. 1030 cm^3 = _____ mL

23. 30000 mL = _____ m^3

24. 120 L = _____ cm^3

Skills Practice Worksheets

The following 36 blackline masters are worksheets for extra skills practice. Each one provides additional exercises for two to four consecutive lessons in the text. The exercises have been carefully modeled after the Examples, Try This and A-level Exercises found in the student text.

You will find these worksheets helpful for students needing extra practice on fundamental concepts. These worksheets could also be incorporated within the context of a chapter or a cumulative review.

1-1 _____ Evaluate.

1. $5a$ for $a = 15$ _____

2. $m - n$ for $m = 17$ and $n = 3$ _____

3. $\frac{w}{z}$ for $w = 42$ and $z = 7$ _____

4. $\frac{3x}{t}$ for $x = 5$ and $t = 35$ _____

5. $\frac{3 + y}{x}$ for $x = 3$ and $y = 9$ _____

6. $\frac{p - q}{6}$ for $p = 13$ and $q = 7$ _____

Simplify.

7. $16 \div 4 + 1$ _____

8. $13 - 12 \div 3$ _____

9. $2 + 7 \times 3$ _____

10. $9 \div 3 + 4 \times 5$ _____

11. $52 \div 13 + 9$ _____

12. $2 + 8 \div 4 - 1$ _____

1-2 _____ Simplify.

13. $\frac{12}{21}$ _____

14. $\frac{54}{9}$ _____

15. $\frac{a}{3ac}$ _____

16. $\frac{2w}{6wz}$ _____

17. $\frac{45s}{5t}$ _____

18. $\frac{17xy}{2xz}$ _____

Write an equivalent expression.

19. $4 + m$ _____

20. $9y$ _____

21. $3a + 5$ _____

Write an equivalent expression. Use the indicated name for 1.

22. $\frac{2}{3}$ Use $\frac{5}{5}$ for 1. _____

23. $\frac{m}{7}$ Use $\frac{n}{n}$ for 1. _____

1-3 _____ Give the meaning of each expression.

24. 16^5 _____

25. y^4 _____

26. $7a^3$ _____

Write using exponential notation.

27. $n \cdot n \cdot 2 \cdot n \cdot n$ _____

28. $5 \cdot c \cdot c \cdot c \cdot c$ _____

29. $t \cdot t \cdot t \cdot t \cdot t$ _____

30. $6 \cdot a \cdot a$ _____

Evaluate each expression.

31. a^3 for $a = 9$ _____

32. $(3m)^2$ for $m = 4$ _____

33. g^1 for $g = 1$ _____

34. c^7 for $c = 1$ _____

35. $(5t)^4$ for $t = 0$ _____

36. $2w^2$ for $w = 5$ _____

37. $5n^3$ for $n = 2$ _____

38. y^8 for $y = 1$ _____

39. $4z^3$ for $z = 0$ _____

1-4 Calculate.

1. $(3 \cdot 5)^3$ _____
2. $3 \cdot 5^3$ _____
3. $(4 - 1)^2$ _____

4. $2 + 9^2$ _____
5. $(2 + 9)^2$ _____
6. $(10 - 9)^5$ _____

7. $6 \cdot 5^2$ _____
8. $(6 \cdot 5)^2$ _____
9. $10 - 3^2$ _____

Evaluate each expression.

10. $2y^2 + 4$ for $y = 2$ _____
11. $(5a)^2 - 100$ for $a = 2$ _____

12. $t(9 + t)$ for $t = 11$ _____
13. $(n + 4) \cdot (5 - n)$ for $n = 4$ _____

14. $\dfrac{m^2 + 15}{2m}$ for $m = 5$ _____
15. $\dfrac{3y + 12}{2y}$ for $y = 4$ _____

Use the associative properties to write an equivalent expression.

16. $4 \cdot (a \cdot b)$ _____
17. $(m + n) + 7$ _____
18. $(3 \cdot y) \cdot z$ _____

Use the commutative and associative properties to write three equivalent expressions.

19. $(7 + s) + t$ _____
20. $4 \cdot (y \cdot z)$ _____

21. $(m \cdot n) \cdot 5$ _____
22. $a + (2 + b)$ _____

23. $a \cdot 3 \cdot b$ _____
24. $(y + 7) + z$ _____

1-5 Use the distributive property to write an equivalent expression.

25. $5(5 + c)$ _____
26. $8(y + 2)$ _____
27. $(m + 1)9$ _____

28. $3(2a + 5)$ _____
29. $4(y + 3z)$ _____
30. $(2a + 3b)4$ _____

Factor and check by multiplying.

31. $9y + 21$ _____
32. $14a + 35b$ _____
33. $3x + 21y + 12z$ _____

34. $7m + 42n$ _____
35. $10c + c$ _____
36. $9 + 21z$ _____

37. $8a + 6b + 10c$ _____
38. $10x + 25y + 30$ _____
39. $36 + 72s + 4t$ _____

Collect like terms.

40. $17c + 6c$ _____
41. $3y + 7x + 5y$ _____

42. $3a^2 + 16 + 9a + 2a^2$ _____
43. $5m + 11n + 11m + 5n$ _____

44. $\dfrac{3}{5}z + \dfrac{2}{5}z + 4z + 9$ _____
45. $\dfrac{3}{10}y + 2y + 7y + \dfrac{7}{10}y$ _____

1-6 _____ Write as an algebraic expression.

1. 6 less than w _____

2. a more than c _____

3. the sum of s and t _____

4. half of z _____

5. m divided among 4 _____

6. t times y _____

7. Let A be Paul's age now. Write an expression for his age five years from now. _____

8. Let E be the amount Sonia earns in an hour. Write an expression for the amount she earns in 40 hours. _____

1-7 _____ State whether each sentence is true, false, or open.

9. $16 - 2 \cdot 4 = 56$ _____

10. $5s = 75$ _____

11. $3^2 + 6 = 15$ _____

Solve for the given replacement set.

12. $7x + 28 = 77$ $\{5, 7, 9\}$ _____

13. $3t^2 - t + 1 = 11$ $\{0, 1, 2, 3\}$ _____

14. $y - 5 + 3y = 25$ $\{5, 6, 7\}$ _____

15. $3x + 5 = 5x - 3$ $\{0, 2, 4, 6\}$ _____

1-8 _____ Solve mentally.

16. $y + 16 = 30$ _____

17. $5s = 75$ _____

18. $a - 17 = 4$ _____

19. $\frac{x}{4} = 9$ _____

20. $\frac{m}{6} = 25$ _____

21. $6c + 5 = 35$ _____

Each pair of equations is equivalent. Tell what was done to the first equation to get the second equation.

22. $3m + 7 = 22$

$3m = 15$ _____

23. $\frac{4x}{9} = 4$

$4x = 36$ _____

1-9 _____ Evaluate.

24. $P = 4s$ for $s = 11.05$ ft (a perimeter formula) _____

25. $T = 0.05p$ for $p = \$25$ (a tax formula) _____

26. $V = lwh$ for $l = 4$ yd, $w = 6$ yd, $h = 15$ ft (a volume formula) _____

27. $D = rt$ for $r = 30$ mi and $t = 1.5$ h (a distance formula) _____

2-1 Name the integer that is suggested by each situation.

1. The Drama Club has 6 new members. _____   **2.** Tom lost 3 pounds. _____

3. Kioki read 164 more pages. _____   **4.** Rachel spent $8.00. _____

5. The temperature fell 15 degrees. _____   **6.** Tai earned $23.00. _____

Write a true sentence using < or >.

7. 3 _____ -1 **8.** -7 _____ -8 **9.** 0 _____ 4   **10.** 7 _____ 2

11. -4 _____ -2 **12.** 0 _____ -1 **13.** 16 _____ -21 **14.** 1 _____ -2

Find the absolute value.

15. $|4|$ _____   **16.** $|-1.7|$ _____   **17.** $|0|$ _____   **18.** $|-8|$ _____

19. $|-5.2|$ _____   **20.** $|0.3|$ _____   **21.** $|-9.1|$ _____   **22.** $|-37|$ _____

2-2 Write a true sentence using < or >.

23. 1.03 _____ 1.30   **24.** -1.65 _____ -1.56 **25.** 0.43 _____ -0.71

26. 1.009 _____ 1.008   **27.** -0.035 _____ -0.036 **28.** 4.2041 _____ 4.2014

29. $\dfrac{2}{5}$ _____ $-\dfrac{1}{3}$ **30.** $\dfrac{1}{8}$ _____ $\dfrac{1}{7}$ **31.** $-\dfrac{3}{7}$ _____ $-\dfrac{2}{5}$

2-3 Add.

32. $0 + (-16)$ _____   **33.** $-7 + 21$ _____   **34.** $4 + (-4)$ _____

35. $\dfrac{1}{5} + \left(-\dfrac{7}{10}\right)$ _____   **36.** $-\dfrac{1}{6} + \dfrac{2}{3}$ _____   **37.** $-\dfrac{3}{4} + \left(-\dfrac{1}{2}\right)$ _____

38. $-3 + 0 + (-7) + 1$ _____   **39.** $19 + (-7) + (-4) + 2$ _____

40. $43 + (-27) + 9 + (-2)$ _____   **41.** $-67 + 21 + 18 + (-4) + (-31)$ _____

Find the additive inverse of each.

42. -8 _____   **43.** 19 _____   **44.** -0.4 _____   **45.** 1.13 _____

Find $-x$ when x is

46. 7 _____   **47.** 1.012 _____   **48.** -25 _____   **49.** -6.7 _____

Find $-(-x)$ when x is

50. 12.9 _____   **51.** -10 _____   **52.** 1.24 _____   **53.** -0.06 _____

12

SKILLS PRACTICE 5

For use with Lessons 2-4–2-6

NAME _____

DATE _____

2-4 Subtract.

1. $16 - 21$ _____
2. $-7 - (-9)$ _____
3. $-6 - 11$ _____

4. $-1.4 - 3.1$ _____
5. $11 - 9.3$ _____
6. $5 - (-1.7)$ _____

7. $-31 - (-14)$ _____
8. $0 - (-1.4)$ _____
9. $-1 - (-6)$ _____

Simplify.

10. $4 - (-7) - 3$ _____
11. $-3 + 6 - (-1)$ _____
12. $-1 + 7 - (-9)$ _____

13. $19 + (-54) - 37$ _____
14. $4 - (-9) - 1$ _____

15. $-3 - (-7) + (-4)$ _____
16. $-5 - (-4) - 3$ _____

17. $2 - 19 - (-6)$ _____
18. $-11 + 16 + (-1)$ _____

Solve.

19. Last night the temperature dropped from 38° F to
 −13° F. How many degrees did the temperature drop? _____

2-5 Multiply.

20. $(-19)(12)(3)$ _____
21. $-6(-25)(-1)$ _____
22. $2(-1.1)(5)$ _____

23. $(-6)(-7)(-4)$ _____
24. $3(-17)(-2)$ _____

25. $-2(9)(-4)$ _____
26. $\left(-\dfrac{1}{2}\right)\left(\dfrac{3}{4}\right)\left(\dfrac{2}{7}\right)$ _____

2-6 Divide. Check your answer.

27. $-54 \div (-6)$ _____
28. $121 \div (-11)$ _____
29. $-240 \div 16$ _____

30. $\dfrac{0}{-3}$ _____
31. $\dfrac{-16}{-2}$ _____
32. $-\dfrac{34}{17}$ _____

33. $-\dfrac{5}{11} \div \dfrac{1}{2}$ _____
34. $\dfrac{2}{3} \div \left(-\dfrac{1}{4}\right)$ _____
35. $-\dfrac{3}{8} \div \left(-\dfrac{2}{3}\right)$ _____

Find the reciprocal.

36. $\dfrac{9}{8}$ _____
37. $-\dfrac{2}{15}$ _____
38. 1.5 _____
39. -2.45 _____

40. $3\dfrac{1}{5}$ _____
41. $-\dfrac{3y}{5}$ _____
42. $\dfrac{7}{2m}$ _____
43. $-\dfrac{1}{5c}$ _____

Rewrite each division as multiplication.

44. $-2 \div 5$ _____
45. $-\dfrac{2}{3}$ _____
46. $\dfrac{4m}{5}$ _____
47. $-\dfrac{2}{3a}$ _____

2-7   Multiply.

1. $-9(x + 2y - 3)$ _____   **2.** $3(2a + b - 3c)$ _____

3. $1.5(45 - 7t)$ _____   **4.** $-2(-3w + 7y - 9z)$ _____

Factor.

5. $16m - 28n$ _____   **6.** $3a - 81c$ _____   **7.** $63v - 7w + 28$ _____

8. $tx - 13t$ _____   **9.** $1.2c - 12$ _____   **10.** $12c - 24d + 8$ _____

What are the terms of each expression?

11. $3a - 19$ _____   **12.** $3x - 4y + 5$ _____

13. $5t - 11s - 2r$ _____   **14.** $2a + 3b - 27c$ _____

Collect like terms.

15. $3a + c - 5a - 19$ _____   **16.** $y - 17y - 31 + 8y$ _____

17. $12s - 7t - 15s + 9t$ _____   **18.** $2m - n - n - 3n$ _____

2-8   Rename each additive inverse without parentheses.

19. $-(3x + 5y)$ _____   **20.** $-(-2a + 3b)$ _____   **21.** $-(7m - 3n)$ _____

Simplify.

22. $6a - (3a + 7c)$ _____   **23.** $15m - (5n - 8m)$ _____

24. $3x + 4y - 2(9x - 3y)$ _____   **25.** $y - 4(3x - 5y)$ _____

26. $-(3s + 2t) - 2(t + s)$ _____   **27.** $2(x - 1) - 4 + 3(3x)$ _____

2-9   Write an equation that can be used to solve the problem.

28. In two days Lupe hiked 65 km. She hiked 34.3 km the
first day. How far did she hike the second day?   _____

29. Dan earns $3 for every lawn he mows. How many
lawns must he mow to earn $54?   _____

30. Tania sold three times as many tickets as Michele.
Michele sold 16 tickets. How many did Tania sell?   _____

3-1   Solve.

1. $a + 17 = 4$ _____   **2.** $n - 9 = 162$ _____   **3.** $60 = 15 - c$ _____

4. $m + \dfrac{2}{5} = \dfrac{1}{2}$ _____   **5.** $b - \dfrac{1}{3} = \dfrac{3}{4}$ _____   **6.** $y + \dfrac{3}{5} = \dfrac{1}{8}$ _____

Translate to an equation and solve.

7. A number increased by 36 is 15. Find the number. _____

8. A number decreased by 83 is 46. Find the number. _____

9. A number is 2.25 less than 1.80. Find the number. _____

10. Rico delivered 292 newspapers to homes this week.
This was 17 more newspapers than last week. How
many newspapers did he deliver last week?   _____

3-2   Solve.

11. $12m = 492$ _____   **12.** $9c = -1053$ _____   **13.** $-182 = -13w$ _____

14. $-\dfrac{x}{8} = -11$ _____   **15.** $\dfrac{3}{5}y = 75$ _____   **16.** $-\dfrac{t}{12} = \dfrac{2}{3}$ _____

Translate to an equation and solve.

17. A number multiplied by 16 is 240. Find the number. _____

18. Thirty-two times a number is -288. Find the number. _____

19. Nancy bought a box of twelve brackets for $11.52.
What was the cost of a single bracket?   _____

20. Shuana bought a skirt on sale for $28.00. That is 80%
of the regular price. What is the regular price?   _____

3-3   Solve.

21. $3x - 1 = 11$ _____   **22.** $4w + 5 = -7$ _____

23. $-2t - 9 = -25$ _____   **24.** $-c + 65 = 54$ _____

25. $3m + 5m = -40$ _____   **26.** $9a - 7a = 4$ _____

27. $2(3y + 1) = -16$ _____   **28.** $3(5 - m) = 27$ _____

29. $3x + 2\left(\dfrac{1}{2}x - x\right) = 4$ _____   **30.** $4\left(\dfrac{1}{5}a - \dfrac{1}{2}\right) + \dfrac{1}{2}a = 11$ _____

3-4   Write as an algebraic expression.

1. 7 less than 4 times a number _____

2. 11 more than half a number _____

3. 5 more than the product of a number and 3 _____

4. $\frac{1}{2}$ the difference of a number and 15 _____

5. The quarterback completed 8 more than half of the passes he attempted. Let $p =$ the number of passes attempted. Write an expression for the number of passes completed.

_____

Solve.

6. Mr. Engen rented a car for $35.00 a day and $0.45 a mile. He had the car for two days and paid $166.75. How many miles did he drive?

_____

7. Nora divided 315 cans equally among 26 cartons and had 3 cans left over. How many cans were in each carton?

_____

8. At Max's Restaurant the cost of a child's dinner is $3.00 less than the cost of an adult dinner. You bought four children's dinners and paid $18.00. Find the cost of an adult dinner.

_____

9. The final exam had three times as many points as the first test, plus a bonus question worth 25 points. The final exam was worth 160 points (including the bonus). How many points was the first test worth?

_____

3-5   Solve.

10. $3x - 7 = x - 9$ _____

11. $4c + 5 = 6c - 1$ _____

12. $2y + 7 = 5y - 8$ _____

13. $10 + 8z = z - 4$ _____

14. $2(3x + 1) = 9x - 1$ _____

15. $2a + (5a - 13) = 47$ _____

16. $3(y + 7) = 2(y + 9)$ _____

17. $3(m - 5) + 1 = 2(m + 1) - 9$ _____

18. $\frac{2}{3} + x = -\frac{5}{2} - \frac{5}{6}$ _____

19. $\frac{1}{2}x + \frac{3}{2}x = x + \frac{9}{2} - \frac{1}{2}x$ _____

20. $5 - \frac{3}{4}y = \frac{5}{3}y + \frac{1}{6}$ _____

21. $\frac{3}{2}x + \frac{1}{5}x = \frac{11}{6}x - \frac{2}{15}$ _____

22. $1.3y - 41 = 3y - 17 - 4.1y$ _____

23. $0.37 + 1.1m = 2.65m - 1.18$ _____

16

SKILLS PRACTICE 9

For use with Lessons 3-7—3-10

NAME _____

DATE _____

3-7   Solve.

1. $A = 2bc$, for b _____

2. $A = 2bc$, for c _____

3. $R = \frac{s}{t}$, for s _____

4. $R = \frac{s}{t}$, for t _____

5. $W = 3y + 3z$, for y _____

6. $W = 3y + 3z$, for z _____

3-8   Solve.

7. $|a| = 6$ _____

8. $|-5| = |c|$ _____

9. $|m| = |-2| + |-1|$ _____

10. $3|y| = 12$ _____

11. $-2|n| + 1 = -5$ _____

12. $|z| = |-5| + |8|$ _____

3-9   Solve.

13. $\frac{52}{4} = \frac{m}{5}$ _____

14. $\frac{2}{7} = \frac{6}{c}$ _____

15. $\frac{105}{168} = \frac{r}{8}$ _____

16. $\frac{8}{a} = \frac{21}{42}$ _____

17. $\frac{t}{9} = \frac{10}{15}$ _____

18. $\frac{3}{5} = \frac{21}{y}$ _____

19. The ratio of boys to girls on the swim team is 5 to 4. How many girls are on the team if there are 65 boys?

_____

20. Mitch can type 4 pages in 15 minutes. At this rate, how many pages can he type in 2 hours?

_____

21. Three inches on a map represent 100 miles. The distance on the map between two cities is $7\frac{1}{2}$ inches. What is the actual distance between the cities?

_____

22. A survey found that 60 out of every 85 people in a city take public transportation to work. Out of 595 people, how many take public transportation to work?

_____

3-10   Write as a decimal.

23. 19% _____

24. 130% _____

25. 0.05% _____

26. 1.65% _____

27. 24% _____

Express as a percent.

28. $\frac{3}{5}$ _____

29. $\frac{7}{10}$ _____

30. $\frac{10}{8}$ _____

31. $\frac{1}{20}$ _____

32. $\frac{3}{2}$ _____

Solve.

33. What percent of 65 is 40? _____

34. What number is 8% of 250? _____

35. What is 120% of 50? _____

36. What percent of 50 is 112? _____

17

SKILLS PRACTICE 10

For use with Lessons 4-1–4-3

NAME _____

DATE _____

4-1 _____ Determine whether the given number is a solution of the inequality.

1. $x \leq 6$ **a.** 4 _____   **b.** 7 _____   **c.** -6 _____   **d.** 6 _____

2. $x > 2$ **a.** 0 _____   **b.** 2 _____   **c.** 3 _____   **d.** 7 _____

3. $x \geq -1$ **a.** -1 _____   **b.** -2 _____   **c.** 0 _____   **d.** 4 _____

4. $x < -3$ **a.** 0 _____   **b.** -4 _____   **c.** 3 _____   **d.** -3 _____

Graph on a number line.

5. $x \leq 0$ _____

6. $x > 2$ _____

7. $x > -1$ _____

8. $x \geq -3$ _____

4-2 _____ Solve and graph the solution.

9. $t - 1 \geq 0$ _____

10. $y + 11 < 6$ _____

11. $m + 3 \leq 5$ _____

12. $3x + 1 - 2x < -1$ _____

13. $a + 1 < -1$ _____

14. $c - 6 > -5$ _____

Solve.

15. $-3a + 16 + 4a > 19$ _____

16. $y - 7 \leq -4$ _____

17. $2 + a < 5$ _____

18. $5c - 4c + 7 < 6$ _____

19. $2y - 9 - y > -6$ _____

20. $-2x + 6 + 3x < 4$ _____

4-3 _____ Solve and graph the solution.

21. $2a \leq -6$ _____

22. $4m < 16$ _____

23. $2c \geq 3$ _____

24. $5t > -10$ _____

25. $3y < -9$ _____

26. $7x \leq -21$ _____

Solve.

27. $-36a \geq 72$ _____

28. $4m \leq -16$ _____

29. $20c < 50$ _____

30. $-2n > -9$ _____

31. $-5y \leq -20$ _____

32. $-6x \leq 30$ _____

4-4 ___ Solve using the addition and multiplication properties.

1. $12a + 5 \leq 101$ _____

2. $6 + 9y < 60$ _____

3. $13 - 4w > 25$ _____

4. $3 + 5y - 2y < 9$ _____

5. $5t + 16 - t \geq 0$ _____

6. $9 - 2x < 5x - 12$ _____

7. $4 - 3n \geq 5n + 20$ _____

8. $4 + 3y \geq 9y - 2$ _____

9. $11 + 2a \leq 5a + 26$ _____

10. $2m - 7 \leq 11 - 4m$ _____

4-5 ___ Translate to an inequality.

11. A number is greater than 10. _____

12. 5 more than a number is less than 3. _____

13. 6 times a number is greater than or equal to -1. _____

14. 13 less than twice a number is at least -4. _____

15. 7 more than half of a number is at most 5. _____

Solve.

16. Stan wants to buy a shirt and a tie and must spend less than $30.00 for both. If the tie costs $7.95, how much can he pay for the shirt?

_____

17. The sum of three consecutive even integers is less than or equal to 126. Find the greatest values of the integers.

_____

18. Farmer Green's hens produced 165 eggs last week and 193 eggs this week. How many eggs must be produced next week to maintain an average of at least 190 eggs a week for the three-week period?

_____

19. Find the greatest possible pair of numbers such that one integer is 5 more than twice the other and the sum is less than 30.

_____

20. Find all numbers such that the sum of the number and 36 is greater than five times the number.

_____

5-1   Simplify. Express using positive exponents.

1. $5^{10} \cdot 5^2$ _____

2. $t^0 \cdot t^5$ _____

3. $4^2 \cdot 4^5 \cdot 4^7$ _____

4. $n^7 \cdot n^3$ _____

5. $a^3 \cdot a^3 \cdot a$ _____

6. $(7x^2y^3)(xy)$ _____

7. $\dfrac{x^{16}y^2}{x^3y}$ _____

8. $\dfrac{(2x)^5}{(2x)^{12}}$ _____

9. $\dfrac{(8x)^5}{(8x)^5}$ _____

Express using positive exponents.

10. 6^{-3} _____

11. x^{-1} _____

12. $3y^{-2}$ _____

13. m^{-4} _____

14. $7y^{-1}$ _____

15. $(5a)^{-1}$ _____

16. 1^{-5} _____

17. x^0 _____

18. $6y^{-3}$ _____

5-2   Simplify.

19. $(2t^4)^3$ _____

20. $(-3x^2)^3$ _____

21. $(a^5b^7c)^6$ _____

22. $(3ab^2)^4$ _____

23. $(-4a^3)^2$ _____

24. $(7x^2y^3z)^2$ _____

25. $\left(\dfrac{x^3}{y^2}\right)^2$ _____

26. $\left(\dfrac{a^2}{2}\right)^4$ _____

27. $\left(\dfrac{3}{5y^2}\right)^2$ _____

5-3   Multiply.

28. $(3m^2)5$ _____

29. $(16y^3)(-7)$ _____

30. $(-3x^5)(x^2)$ _____

31. $(-2a^2)(3a^9)$ _____

32. $(x^2y^5)(xy^2)$ _____

33. $(2a^2b)(5ab)$ _____

Divide.

34. $\dfrac{x^{16}}{x^4}$ _____

35. $\dfrac{t^2}{t^2}$ _____

36. $\dfrac{5m^7}{m^4}$ _____

37. $\dfrac{12x^5}{3x^3}$ _____

38. $\dfrac{4a^3}{4}$ _____

39. $\dfrac{25a^2b^3}{5a}$ _____

5-4   Write using standard notation.

40. 6.781×10^5 _____

41. 2.001×10^{-2} _____

42. 7.61×10^{-5} _____

43. 3.114×10^3 _____

Write using scientific notation.

44. 6,821,000 _____

45. 0.810001 _____

46. 0.00000671 _____

47. 2631 _____

5-5   Identify the terms. Give the coefficient of each term.

1. $a^3 - 2ab + 7a$ _____

2. $-3mn - 11n + 6$ _____

3. $-x^2 + 3y + 9$ _____

4. $-9a^2c - ac + 11c$ _____

Collect like terms.

5. $7y + 16 - 5y$ _____

6. $6x^2 + 11x - x^2 + 1$ _____

7. $3a^2 + 5b^2 - ab - 4a^2 + 2ab - b^2 + 4ab$ _____

Identify the degree of each term and the degree of the polynomial.

8. $3x + 5$ _____

9. $-6x + 1$ _____

10. $-3a^2 + 7a - 19$ _____

11. $x^3y^2 - 37$ _____

12. $5a^2b^3 - 7a^2b^2 + 4ab^3 - 11a + 9$ _____

5-6   Arrange each polynomial in descending order for the variable x.

13. $5x^2 - 7x + 16x^3 - 19 - 5x^5$ _____

14. $10 - x^2y^3 + 7xy - x^5y^2 - 9x^4 + x^3$ _____

15. $-x^2y + x - 17 - 6x^3y^5 + x^4y$ _____

Evaluate each polynomial for $m = 2$ and $n = 3$.

16. $n^2 + 4$ _____

17. $mn - 3$ _____

18. $m^2 + m$ _____

19. $-3m^2 + 16n + 5$ _____

20. $m^2n^2 - mn + 1$ _____

5-7   Add.

21. $(4x^2 + 3x - 9) + (-9x + 10)$ _____

22. $(9x^4 + 5x^2 - 2) + (3x^3 + 3)$ _____

23. $(2x^4 + 5x^2 - 7x - 4) + (-7x^4 - 3x^2 + 7x + 5)$ _____

24. $(14x^3 - 4x^2 - 3) + (9x^2 + 6x - 2)$ _____

25. $(4x^2 + 3x - 1) + (-2x^2 + x + 5)$ _____

26. $(2m^2n + mn) + (3m^2 + m^2n - mn)$ _____

27. $(a^3 - 7ab + 19) + (b^2 - a^3 + 1)$ _____

SKILLS PRACTICE 14

For use with Lessons 5-8–5-11

NAME _____

DATE _____

5-8   Find the additive inverse of each polynomial.

1. $6x^2 + x$ _____   **2.** $17ab - 1$ _____

3. $12a^2b + 2ab^2$ _____   **4.** $4m^3 - 7m + 5$ _____

Subtract.

5. $(3x^2 - 6) - (x^2 + 1)$ _____

6. $(5a^2 - 7a + 1) - (2a^2 + 3a - 6)$ _____

7. $(3m^2n + mn - 5) - (2m^2n - m + 9)$ _____

8. $(11x^2y + 6xy - y^2 + 6) - (4x^2 + 3y^2 - 9)$ _____

9. $(4t^3 + 8t^2 - t + 21) - (3t^2 - 10t)$ _____

5-9   Multiply.

10. $7(12x^2)$ _____   **11.** $(0.2x^2)(0.4x^6)$ _____

12. $2x^2(-x + 12)$ _____   **13.** $-3x^3(x^5 - x)$ _____

14. $6y^9(2y^{20} - 5y^3 - 20)$ _____   **15.** $(a - 4)(a - 8)$ _____

16. $(x + 5)(x - 5)$ _____   **17.** $(9 - 2n)(2n - 9)$ _____

18. $(x^3 - 2)(x^2 - 2)$ _____   **19.** $(4m + 6)(m - 3)$ _____

5-10   Multiply.

20. $(x + 7)(x - 7)$ _____   **21.** $(3x + 5)(3x - 5)$ _____

22. $(t + 9)^2$ _____   **23.** $(2x + 7)^2$ _____

24. $(c - 12)^2$ _____   **25.** $(5 - 2t)^2$ _____

26. $(3m^2 - n)(3m^2 + n)$ _____   **27.** $(2a^2 - 0.3)(2a^2 + 0.3)$ _____

5-11   Multiply.

28. $3a^2(2b^3 - 9b^2 + 6)$ _____

29. $(5m^2 - 3n)^2$ _____

30. $(x - 1)(x^2 - 2x + 1)$ _____

31. $(2a^2 + b)(2a^2 - b)$ _____

32. $(5y^2 + 6)^2$ _____

6-1   Find three factorizations for each monomial.

1. $18a^3b$ _____   **2.** $-8mn^2$ _____   **3.** $15xyz$ _____

Factor.

4. $5x^2 - 15$ _____   **5.** $y^5 + 9y^2$ _____

6. $8a^2 + 10a - 16$ _____   **7.** $3c^4 - 6c^2 - 15c$ _____

8. $4m^4n^2 - 6n$ _____   **9.** $6a^2b^3 - 14abc$ _____

6-2   Which of the following are differences of two squares?

10. $x^2 - 121$ _____   **11.** $4a^2 + 169$ _____   **12.** $x^8 - 5x^2$ _____

13. $100a^2 - 9$ _____   **14.** $m^2 - 24$ _____   **15.** $64 - 25c^2$ _____

Factor.

16. $x^2 - 49$ _____   **17.** $9a^2 - 400$ _____

18. $16c^3 - 9c$ _____   **19.** $y^8 - 4y^2$ _____

20. $5m^2 - 20$ _____   **21.** $64 - 25c^2$ _____

22. $100 - 36n^2$ _____   **23.** $x^6 - 9x^4$ _____

6-3   Which of the following are trinomial squares?

24. $x^2 - 6x - 9$ _____   **25.** $m^2 + 6m + 9$ _____

26. $a^2 + 10a + 25$ _____   **27.** $y^2 + 2y + 1$ _____

28. $c^4 + 8c - 16$ _____   **29.** $t^2 - 10t + 25$ _____

Factor.

30. $x^2 + 16x + 64$ _____   **31.** $n^2 - 20n + 100$ _____

32. $16 - 8a + a^2$ _____   **33.** $c^3 + 16c^2 + 64c$ _____

34. $25m^2 + 30m + 9$ _____   **35.** $4 - 28x + 49x^2$ _____

36. $16y^3 + 48y^2 + 36y$ _____   **37.** $a^4 + 4a^2 + 4$ _____

38. $c^2 + 14c + 49$ _____   **39.** $4y^2 - 16y + 16$ _____

40. $10t^2 - 20t + 10$ _____   **41.** $x^3 + 6x^2 + 9x$ _____

6-4   Factor.

1. $x^2 + 9x + 14$ _____   2. $y^2 - 15y + 54$ _____

3. $a^2 - 3a - 18$ _____   4. $m^2 + 23m - 24$ _____

5. $a^2 + 2a - 3$ _____   6. $t^2 + 8t + 15$ _____

7. $y^2 - 10y + 16$ _____   8. $a^2 + 2a - 24$ _____

9. $x^2 + x - 42$ _____   10. $n^2 - 12n + 35$ _____

11. $m^2 + 5m + 6$ _____   12. $a^2 + 4a - 5$ _____

13. $t^2 - 7t + 12$ _____   14. $y^2 + 10y + 21$ _____

6-5   Factor.

15. $2x^2 - 13x - 45$ _____   16. $2y^2 - 10y + 8$ _____

17. $15 - 2c - c^2$ _____   18. $8a^2 + 22a + 15$ _____

19. $21 + m - 10m^2$ _____   20. $18n^2 + 33n - 6$ _____

21. $3y^2 - 20y + 12$ _____   22. $40x^2 + 10x - 15$ _____

23. $a^3 - 8a^2 + 16a$ _____   24. $84 - 2c - 2c^2$ _____

25. $2x^2 - 3x - 2$ _____   26. $3a^2 - 10a + 3$ _____

27. $2x^2 - 12x + 10$ _____   28. $5y^2 + 25y + 30$ _____

6-6   Factor by grouping.

29. $x^3 - 2x^2 + 3x - 6$ _____

30. $y^3 - y + 3y^2 - 3$ _____

31. $4a^3 + 28a^2 + a + 7$ _____

32. $8m^3 - 20m^2 - 6m + 15$ _____

33. $t^3 + 2t^2 - 7t - 14$ _____

34. $c^3 + 3c^2 - 9c - 27$ _____

35. $y^3 + y + 2y^2 + 2$ _____

36. $n^3 - 2n^2 + 4n - 8$ _____

6-7   Factor.

1. $x^2 + 2x - 3$ _____

2. $4y^2 - 81$ _____

3. $7a^2 - 33a - 10$ _____

4. $4c^2 - 12c - 40$ _____

5. $m^5 + 7m^4 + 6m^3$ _____

6. $t^3 + 4t^2 + 4t + 16$ _____

7. $n^5 - 4n^3 - 5n$ _____

8. $x^2 - 11x + 28$ _____

9. $4c^2 - 25$ _____

10. $3x^2 - 5x - 2$ _____

11. $10x^2 + x - 3$ _____

12. $y^5 + y^4 - 5y^3 - 5y^2$ _____

13. $a^2 + 15a + 26$ _____

14. $12x^2 - 3$ _____

15. $m^3 - 6m^2 - 27m$ _____

16. $t^7 - 9t^5$ _____

6-8   Solve.

17. $(a - 5)(a + 2) = 0$ _____

18. $(c + 1)(c + 7) = 0$ _____

19. $x(x - 3) = 0$ _____

20. $(2m + 1)(m + 4) = 0$ _____

21. $5y(3y + 11) = 0$ _____

22. $(0.5t - 2)(0.4t + 6) = 0$ _____

23. $x^2 + 5x + 6 = 0$ _____

24. $y^2 - 11y + 28 = 0$ _____

25. $16t^2 = 64$ _____

26. $a^2 + 2a = 15$ _____

27. $y^2 + 3y = 36 - 2y$ _____

28. $m^2 + 3m = 10m - 6$ _____

6-9   Translate to an equation and solve.

29. The product of two consecutive odd whole numbers is 143. Find the numbers.

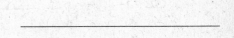

30. Twenty more than the square of a number is twelve times the number. Find the number.

31. The product of three more than a number times two less than the number is fourteen. Find the number.

32. The sum of the squares of two consecutive odd positive integers is 202. Find the numbers.

_____

33. The product of two consecutive even whole numbers is 288. Find the numbers.

_____

7-1

Use the graph to plot these points.

1. (1, 2) **2.** (−2, 3) **3.** (0, 4)

4. (−4, −1) **5.** (2, −1) **6.** (−3, 0)

7. (3, 1) **8.** (−2, −3) **9.** (−3, 3)

10. (3, −2) **11.** (−1, −1) **12.** (1, −4)

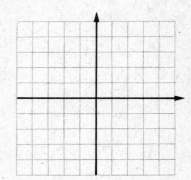

In which quadrant is each point located?

13. (−7, 3) _____ **14.** (6, 3) _____

15. (9, −1) _____ **16.** (−5, −10) _____

17. (1, 7) _____ **18.** (−5, 8) _____

Find the coordinates of each point.

19. A _____ **20.** B _____ **21.** C _____

22. D _____ **23.** E _____ **24.** F _____

25. G _____ **26.** H _____ **27.** J _____

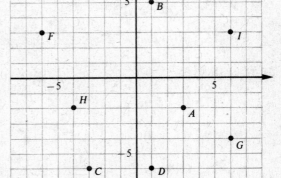

7-2

Determine whether the given point is a solution of $x + 2y = 5$.

28. (1, 2) _____ **29.** (3, −4) _____ **30.** (−3, 4) _____

Determine whether the given point is a solution of $6y = 4x − 3$.

31. $\left(-\dfrac{1}{3}, -\dfrac{13}{18}\right)$ _____ **32.** $\left(\dfrac{1}{2}, -\dfrac{1}{6}\right)$ _____ **33.** $\left(\dfrac{1}{8}, \dfrac{5}{12}\right)$ _____

Make a table of solutions and graph each equation.

34. $3x − y = 4$ **35.** $y − 5 = 2x$ **36.** $x + y = 1$

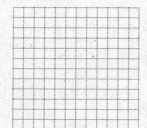 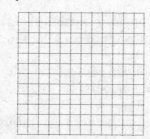 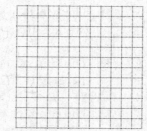

26

SKILLS PRACTICE 19

For use with Lessons 7-3—7-4

NAME _____

DATE _____

7-3 ___ Graph using intercepts.

1. $y = x - 2$

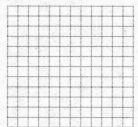

2. $2x + 4 = y$

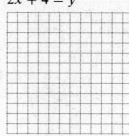

3. $y - 2x = 5$

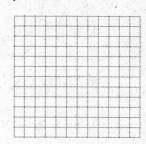

4. $5y + 5x = 10$

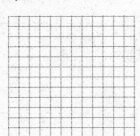

5. $6y - 3x = 9$

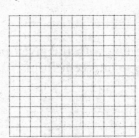

6. $2y + 4x = 14$

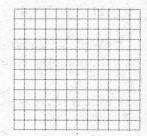

Graph.

7. $x = 2$

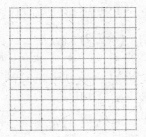

8. $y = -\dfrac{7}{2}$

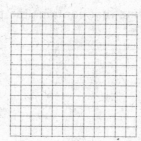

9. $x = -\dfrac{1}{2}$

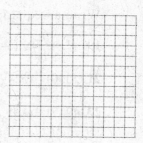

7-4 ___ Find the slopes, if they exist, of the lines containing these points.

10. $(3, -5)$ $(1, -1)$ _____

11. $(5, 4)$ $(-7, 4)$ _____

12. $(8, 4)$ $(9, 10)$ _____

13. $(-3, 2)$ $(-3, 5)$ _____

14. $(6, -2)$ $(-3, 4)$ _____

15. $(7, 1)$ $(-3, 5)$ _____

16. $\left(\dfrac{5}{2}, \dfrac{3}{4}\right)$ $\left(2, \dfrac{1}{2}\right)$ _____

17. $\left(\dfrac{3}{5}, \dfrac{1}{8}\right)$ $\left(2\dfrac{1}{10}, \dfrac{5}{8}\right)$ _____

7-5   Find the slope and the *y*-intercept of each line.

1. $5y = -4x + 5$ _____

2. $6x - 14 = y$ _____

3. $x + 3y = 12$ _____

4. $y = -4x - \dfrac{1}{2}$ _____

5. $\dfrac{y}{4} = 2x$ _____

6. $\dfrac{x}{2} - \dfrac{y}{4} = \dfrac{1}{3}$ _____

7. $8y = 2x + 20$ _____

8. $12y = -8x - 16$ _____

9. $4y + 5x = 24$ _____

10. $1.2x + 0.6y = 1.8$ _____

11. $y + 7 = 4x$ _____

12. $y + 3x = 1$ _____

7-6   Write an equation for each line with the given point and slope.
       Express the equation in slope-intercept form.

13. $(1, 3), m = 4$ _____

14. $(4, 2), m = \dfrac{1}{3}$ _____

15. $(2, 4), m = 3$ _____

16. $(4, 0), m = -\dfrac{2}{5}$ _____

17. $(1, 2), m = -1$ _____

18. $(0, 9), m = 2$ _____

Write an equation for the line that contains the given pairs of points.

19. $(1, -7)$ $(-2, 8)$ _____

20. $(4, -1)$ $(-2, 2)$ _____

21. $(3, 0)$ $(5, -4)$ _____

22. $(1, 2)$ $(3, 0)$ _____

23. $(2, 7)$ $(-1, -8)$ _____

24. $(0, -1)$ $(2, 3)$ _____

7-8   Determine whether the graphs of the equations are parallel lines.

25. $y = 3x + 1$
$y - 3x = 7$ _____

26. $5y = x + 2$
$y - 2 = 5x$ _____

27. $x = -2$
$x = 1$ _____

Determine whether the graphs of the equations are perpendicular lines.

28. $2y = x - 11$
$y + 3 = 2x$ _____

29. $2x - 5y = 4$
$5x + 2y = 10$ _____

30. $5x + 3y = 2$
$3x - 5y = 8$ _____

Determine whether the graphs of the equations are parallel, perpendicular, or neither.

31. $3y + 2x = 6$
$y = 7 - 3x$ _____

32. $2x - 4y = 3$
$3x - 6y = 8$ _____

33. $y + x = 5$
$x - y = -4$ _____

8-1 _____   Determine whether $(-4, 5)$ is a solution of the system of equations.

1. $x + y = 1$
$2x + y = 3$ _____

2. $2x + 2y = 0$
$4x + 2y = 6$ _____

3. $2x + 2y = 2$
$2x + y = -3$ _____

4. $x + 2y = -14$
$2x + y = 3$ _____

Solve by graphing.

5. $x + y = 6$
$x - y = 4$

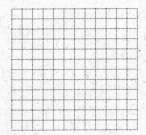

6. $3x + 4y = 20$
$3x - 2y = 8$

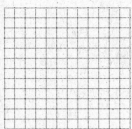

7. $x + y = 3$
$2x - y = 2$

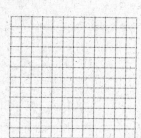

8. $3x + 5y = 2$
$6x + 4y = -2$

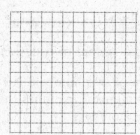

8-2 _____   Solve using the substitution method.

9. $y = 5 - x$
$2x + 3y = 12$ _____

10. $x + y = 6$
$x + 4y = 3$ _____

Translate to a system of equations and solve.

11. The sum of two numbers is 141. One number is 37 more than the other. Find the numbers.

_____

12. Find two numbers whose sum is 54 and whose difference is 28.

_____

13. The difference between two numbers is 9. Three times the larger number is six times the smaller. What are the numbers?

_____

14. The difference between two numbers is 9. Three times the smaller plus five times the larger is 61. What are the numbers?

_____

8-3   Solve using the addition method.

1. $2x + y = 1$
$x - y = 11$ _____

2. $3x - 2y = 12$
$5x + 2y = 4$ _____

3. $2x + 5y = 2$
$3x - 2y = 3$ _____

4. $6x + 3y = 0$
$8x + 5y = 8$ _____

5. $x + y = 6$
$x - y = 10$ _____

6. $-x - y = 15$
$4x - y = -5$ _____

Solve.

7. $x - 3y = 9$
$3x + y = 7$ _____

8. $x + y = 4$
$2x - y = 5$ _____

9. $x + 2y = 1$
$2x - 3y = 16$ _____

10. $3x - y = -13$
$x + 5y = 17$ _____

11. $2x + 3y = 12$
$y - 2x = 4$ _____

12. $5x + 2y = 22$
$x + 2y = 14$ _____

13. $y = 7 - 2x$
$5y = -3x + 7$ _____

14. $x - y = 9$
$3x + y = 11$ _____

Translate to a system of equations and solve.

15. The sum of two numbers is 14. Six times the first number minus three times the second number is 3. Find the numbers.

_____

16. The sum of two numbers is 57.4. One number is six times the other. Find the numbers.

_____

17. The sum of two numbers is 56. The difference is 22. Find the numbers.

_____

8-4   Translate to a system of equations and solve.

18. Tanisha has 70 coins, all quarters and dimes. There are 30 more quarters than dimes. Find the number of each type of coin.

_____

19. A mother is 27 years older than her daughter. A year ago, the mother was twice as old as her daughter. How old is each now?

_____

20. Two bagels and a glass of juice cost $1.20. Three bagels and two glasses of juice cost $2.05. Find the cost of a bagel and the cost of a glass of juice.

_____

SKILLS PRACTICE 23

For use with Lessons 8-5—8-6

NAME _____

DATE _____

8-5   Solve.

1. A fishing boat traveled 3 hours against a 6 km/hr current. The return trip took only 2 hours. Find the speed of the boat in still water.

_____

2. An airplane flew for 3 hours with a tail wind of 40 km/hr. The return flight against the same wind took 4 hours. Find the speed of the airplane in still air.

_____

3. An airplane flew for 6 hours with a tail wind of 60 km/hr. The return flight against the same wind took 8 hours. Find the speed of the airplane in still air.

_____

4. The speed of a stream is 3 km/hr. A boat travels 4 km upstream in the same time it takes to travel 10 km downstream. What is the speed of the boat in still water?

_____

8-6   Solve.

5. A theater has 650 seats. After one sell-out performance, the theater made $11,600. If orchestra seats cost $20 each and balcony seats cost $12, how many orchestra and balcony seats are there in the theater?

_____

6. The sum of the digits of a two-digit number is 9. If the digits are reversed, the new number is 27 less than the original. Find the original number.

_____

7. Rico's collection of quarters and dimes contains $32.85. There are 171 coins in all. How many quarters and how many dimes are in Rico's collection?

_____

8. Airline fares for a flight from Elmwood to Palmdale are $85 for first class and $60 for coach class. On Friday, 79 passengers paid a total of $5290 to fly from Elmwood to Palmdale. How many of each type of ticket were sold?

_____

9-1 ___ Write using (a) roster notation and (b) set-builder notation.

1. The set N of whole numbers less than 10

   _____

2. The set P of prime numbers between 50 and 80

   _____

3. The set M of positive multiples of 7 that are less than or equal to 85

   _____

4. The set S of integers that are perfect squares less than 100

   _____

5. The set F of positive factors of 36

   _____

Let $A = \{1, 3, 5, 7, 9, 11, 13, 15\}$, $B = \{0, 3, 6, 9, 12, 15\}$, and $C = \{0, 2, 4, 6, 8, 10, 12, 14\}$. Find each of the following.

6. $A \cap B$ _____   7. $B \cup C$ _____

8. $A \cap C$ _____   9. $A \cup B$ _____

10. $B \cap C$ _____   11. $A \cup C$ _____

12. Let E be the set of positive integers and T be the set of perfect squares. Find $E \cap T$ and $E \cup T$.

    _____

9-2 ___ Solve and graph.

13. $-1 < x + 1 < 6$ _____

14. $1 < 2y + 5 \leq 9$ _____

15. $3 \leq 5x + 3 \leq 8$ _____

Solve and graph.

16. $2x + 3 < 5$ or $x - 3 \geq 0$ _____

17. $3x - 5 < 1$ or $2x - 8 > 8$ _____

18. $5x + 10 < 0$ or $3x - 3 > x - 1$ _____

9-3 _____ Solve.

1. $|x + 5| = 16$ _____

2. $|x - 7| = 4$ _____

3. $|2x - 1| = 5$ _____

4. $|3x + 2| = 14$ _____

5. $|x + 1| = -3$ _____

6. $|2a + 1.6| = 4.2$ _____

7. $|5m + 1| = 13$ _____

8. $|2x + 14| = 8$ _____

9. $|y + 4| = -9$ _____

10. $|0.5m + 1| = 3$ _____

9-4 _____ Graph on a number line.

11. $|x| < 3$

12. $|y| \leq 5$

13. $|m| \leq 1.5$

Solve and graph.

14. $|2x + 6| \leq 8$ _____

15. $|x + 2| < 3$ _____

16. $|x - 3| \leq 7$ _____

17. $|4y - 1| < 11$ _____

18. $|2a + 5| < 1$ _____

Graph on a number line.

19. $|x| > 2.5$

20. $|y| \geq 2$

21. $|c| \geq 4.5$

Solve and graph.

22. $|2y + 6| \geq 8$ _____

23. $|3a| \geq 9$ _____

24. $|y + 4| > 2$ _____

25. $|4m - 3| > 9$ _____

26. $|t - 4| > 1$ _____

9-5   Determine whether the given point is a solution of the inequality.

1. $(1, -4)$; $4x - 5y < 12$ _____

2. $(-4, 2)$; $2x + y < -5$ _____

3. $(-3, 2)$; $5x - 4y \leq 13$ _____

4. $(3, -6)$; $4x + 2y \geq 0$ _____

5. $(8, 14)$; $2y - 3x > 5$ _____

6. $(7, 20)$; $3x - y > -1$ _____

Graph each inequality.

7. $y \geq x + 1$

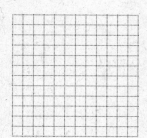

8. $y < x + 2$

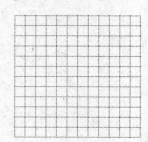

9. $x - y > 4$

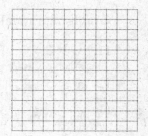

9-6   Solve these systems by graphing.

10. $y > 2x$
    $x + y > -1$

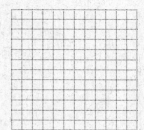

11. $x + y \geq 2$
    $x \leq 2$

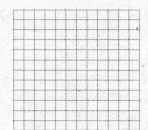

12. $y - 2x > -1$
    $y - 2x < 2$

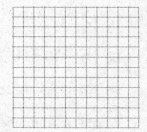

13. $y > -\dfrac{1}{2}$
    $y > x + 2$

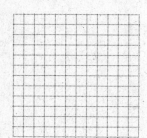

14. $3y - 2x > 6$
    $x + y \leq 2$

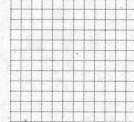

15. $2y + x > 2$
    $3y \leq 6$

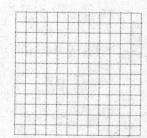

SKILLS PRACTICE 27

For use with Lessons 10-1–10-3

NAME _____

DATE _____

10-1   Simplify.

1. $\dfrac{x^2 - 1}{2x^2 - x - 1}$ _____

2. $\dfrac{6x^2 + 4x}{2x^2 + 4x}$ _____

3. $\dfrac{y^2 + 3y + 2}{y^2 - 1}$ _____

4. $\dfrac{x^2 - 16}{x^2 - 6x + 8}$ _____

5. $\dfrac{2x^2 - 2}{4x^2 - 4}$ _____

6. $\dfrac{x^2 - 10x + 25}{x - 5}$ _____

10-2   Multiply. Simplify the product.

7. $\dfrac{2x}{x + 4} \cdot \dfrac{x - 1}{3}$ _____

8. $\dfrac{x - 3}{x + 4} \cdot \dfrac{x + 3}{x + 4}$ _____

9. $\dfrac{4}{2x - 3} \cdot \dfrac{-5}{4x + 6}$ _____

10. $\dfrac{x + 2}{x^2 - 4} \cdot \dfrac{x - 2}{x^2 + 4}$ _____

11. $\dfrac{-3x^2}{x + 1} \cdot \dfrac{x + 1}{6x}$ _____

12. $\dfrac{2 - t}{3 + t} \cdot \dfrac{4 + t}{t}$ _____

13. $\dfrac{x^2 + 3x - 10}{x^2 - 10x + 25} \cdot \dfrac{x - 5}{x - 2}$ _____

14. $\dfrac{t^2 - 16}{t^2 - 2t} \cdot \dfrac{t - 2}{t - 4}$ _____

15. $\dfrac{6x^2}{6x^2 + 9x + 3} \cdot \dfrac{6x + 3}{2x}$ _____

16. $\dfrac{x^2 + 5x + 4}{x^2 + 3x + 2} \cdot \dfrac{x^2 - 3x - 10}{x^2 - x - 20}$ _____

17. $\dfrac{x^2 + 4x - 12}{4x - 6} \cdot \dfrac{8x^2 - 18}{5x + 30}$ _____

18. $\dfrac{a^2 - a - 12}{a^2 - 5a + 4} \cdot \dfrac{a^2 + 2a - 3}{a^2 + a - 6}$ _____

10-3   Divide and simplify.

19. $\dfrac{3y + 15}{y} \div \dfrac{y + 5}{y}$ _____

20. $\dfrac{6x + 12}{x} \div \dfrac{x + 2}{x^3}$ _____

21. $\dfrac{y^2 - 9}{y} \div \dfrac{y + 3}{y + 2}$ _____

22. $\dfrac{3x + 12}{x - 4} \div \dfrac{3x}{2x - 8}$ _____

23. $\dfrac{2x - 6}{3} \div \dfrac{x - 3}{12}$ _____

24. $\dfrac{x^2 + 6x + 9}{x + 6} \div \dfrac{x + 3}{x + 6}$ _____

25. $\dfrac{y^2 + 6y + 8}{y - 1} \div \dfrac{y^2 - 4}{y - 1}$ _____

26. $\dfrac{x^2 + 2x}{4x + 12} \div \dfrac{x^2 - 2x - 8}{x^2 - x - 12}$ _____

27. $\dfrac{x^2 - 2x}{x^2 + 2x - 8} \div \dfrac{x^2 + 5x}{x^2 + 7x + 12}$ _____

28. $\dfrac{6x^3}{x^2 - 3x} \div \dfrac{3x^2}{x^2 - 9}$ _____

29. $\dfrac{x^2 - 3x}{x^2 - 5x + 6} \div \dfrac{2x + 4}{x^2 - 4}$ _____

30. $\dfrac{x^2 + x - 6}{x^2 - 4x - 21} \div \dfrac{x^2 - x - 2}{x^2 - 8x + 7}$ _____

10-4   Add or subtract. Simplify.

1. $\dfrac{2x+1}{x+2} + \dfrac{3}{x+2}$ _____

2. $\dfrac{9a}{5a+2} - \dfrac{4a-2}{5a+2}$ _____

3. $\dfrac{4x+5}{x+3} - \dfrac{x-2}{x+3}$ _____

4. $\dfrac{4y+3}{y-2} - \dfrac{y-2}{y-2}$ _____

5. $\dfrac{x-5y}{x+y} + \dfrac{x+7y}{x+y}$ _____

6. $\dfrac{4m+5}{m-2} + \dfrac{5-3m}{m-2}$ _____

10-5   Find the least common multiple (LCM).

7. $x^2 - y^2,\ x + y$ _____

8. $a,\ a+7$ _____

9. $y+4,\ y-5$ _____

10. $2a^2,\ 6a$ _____

11. $12a^2b,\ 8b^2$ _____

12. $6m^3n,\ 9mn^2$ _____

Add and simplify.

13. $\dfrac{1}{a} + \dfrac{a+4}{a^2}$ _____

14. $\dfrac{3x}{x+2} + \dfrac{12x}{x^2-4}$ _____

15. $\dfrac{4xy}{x^2-y^2} + \dfrac{x-y}{x+y}$ _____

16. $\dfrac{2x}{x-5} + \dfrac{x+1}{5-x}$ _____

17. $\dfrac{y}{y^2-y-20} + \dfrac{2}{y+4}$ _____

18. $\dfrac{5x}{x^2-1} + \dfrac{3}{x-1}$ _____

Subtract and simplify.

19. $\dfrac{7y-1}{6y} - \dfrac{2y+1}{3y}$ _____

20. $\dfrac{4}{x+2} - \dfrac{5}{x-2}$ _____

21. $\dfrac{5}{x^2+x-6} - \dfrac{6}{x^2+2x-8}$ _____

22. $\dfrac{3}{x-4} - \dfrac{3}{x+2}$ _____

23. $\dfrac{a}{a+1} - \dfrac{1}{a-1}$ _____

24. $\dfrac{x^2}{5} - \dfrac{5}{x^2}$ _____

10-6   Solve.

25. $\dfrac{5}{4} - \dfrac{5}{9} = \dfrac{x}{12}$ _____

26. $\dfrac{2}{3} = \dfrac{1}{y} + \dfrac{5}{8}$ _____

27. $\dfrac{1}{5} = \dfrac{x-6}{x+6}$ _____

28. $\dfrac{9}{x-3} = \dfrac{2x}{x-3}$ _____

29. $\dfrac{1}{2x} = \dfrac{1}{x+3}$ _____

30. $\dfrac{5x}{x-3} = \dfrac{2x}{x+1}$ _____

SKILLS PRACTICE 29
For use with Lessons 10-7—10-10

NAME _____

DATE _____

<u>10-7</u>   Solve.

1. The reciprocal of 4 less than a number is twice the reciprocal of the number itself. What is the numer? _____

2. It takes a new mail carrier 4 hours to deliver the mail on Route A. It takes an experienced mail carrier 3 hours to do the same job. How long would it take if they worked together? _____

<u>10-8</u>   Solve.

3. Solution A is 50 % acid. Solution B is 60% acid. How much of each solution is needed to make a 100 L solution that is 51% acid? _____

4. Fruit drink A is 20% apple juice and fruit drink B is 40% apple juice. How much of each is needed to make 40 liters of drink that is 35% apple juice? _____

5. House Blend coffe is 50% Columbian beans and Special Blend coffee is 80% columbian beans. How much of each should be used to produce 100kg of a blend that is 68% Columbian beans? _____

<u>10-9</u>   Divide.

6. $\left(14x^2 + 28x + 25\right) \div 7$ _____ **7.** $\left(15x^4 - 25x^2 + 12x\right) \div 5x$ _____

8. $\left(12x^5 + 18x^4 - 36x^2\right) \div -3x^2$ _____ **9.** $\left(x^3 + 216\right) \div (x + 6)$ _____

10. $\left(x^3 - 2x^2 + 4x - 8\right) \div (x - 2)$ _____ **11.** $\left(x^2 - 21x + 24\right) \div (x - 6)$ _____

12. $\left(5x^3 + 9x^2 + 18x - 4\right) \div (5x - 1)$ _____ **13.** $\left(x^4 - 1\right) \div (x - 1)$ _____

<u>10-10</u>   Simplify.

14. $\dfrac{1 - \dfrac{9}{25}}{1 - \dfrac{3}{5}}$ _____ **15.** $\dfrac{1 + \dfrac{1}{y}}{y - \dfrac{1}{y}}$ _____

16. $\dfrac{1 + \dfrac{1}{x}}{5}$ _____ **17.** $\dfrac{\dfrac{1}{x}}{1 - \dfrac{1}{x}}$ _____

11-1

Simplify.

1. $\sqrt{64}$ _____   **2.** $-\sqrt{144}$ _____   **3.** $\sqrt{625}$ _____   **4.** $-\sqrt{256}$ _____

5. $-\sqrt{100}$ _____   **6.** $\sqrt{49}$ _____   **7.** $-\sqrt{1}$ _____   **8.** $\sqrt{1}$ _____

Identify each square root as rational or irrational.

9. $\sqrt{48}$ _____   **10.** $\sqrt{10}$ _____   **11.** $\sqrt{36}$ _____   **12.** $\sqrt{144}$ _____

13. $\sqrt{120}$ _____   **14.** $\sqrt{169}$ _____   **15.** $\sqrt{400}$ _____   **16.** $\sqrt{200}$ _____

11-2

Determine the values of x that will make each expression a real number.

17. $\sqrt{x-1}$ _____   **18.** $\sqrt{3x}$ _____   **19.** $\sqrt{2x^2}$ _____   **20.** $\sqrt{x+7}$ _____

21. $\sqrt{x^2+1}$ _____   **22.** $\sqrt{x-10}$ _____   **23.** $\sqrt{2x+1}$ _____   **24.** $\sqrt{3x-5}$ _____

Simplify.

25. $\sqrt{a^2b^2c^2}$ _____   **26.** $\sqrt{(x-2)^2}$ _____   **27.** $\sqrt{(9m)^2}$ _____

28. $\sqrt{(x+1)^2}$ _____   **29.** $\sqrt{(-5c)^2}$ _____   **30.** $\sqrt{49t^2}$ _____

31. $\sqrt{y^2-16y+64}$ _____   **32.** $\sqrt{x^2+6x+9}$ _____

11-3

Factor and simplify. Assume that all variables are nonnegative.

33. $\sqrt{27}$ _____   **34.** $\sqrt{128}$ _____   **35.** $\sqrt{80}$ _____

36. $\sqrt{16t}$ _____   **37.** $\sqrt{64y}$ _____   **38.** $\sqrt{15y^2}$ _____

39. $\sqrt{12a^2}$ _____   **40.** $\sqrt{400y^2}$ _____   **41.** $\sqrt{31y^2}$ _____

42. $\sqrt{250b}$ _____   **43.** $\sqrt{180}$ _____   **44.** $\sqrt{18a^2b^2}$ _____

45. $\sqrt{165}$ _____   **46.** $\sqrt{1000}$ _____   **47.** $\sqrt{75x}$ _____

48. $\sqrt{44m^2}$ _____   **49.** $\sqrt{50a}$ _____   **50.** $\sqrt{60c^2}$ _____

51. $\sqrt{200x}$ _____   **52.** $\sqrt{90x^2}$ _____   **53.** $\sqrt{y^{24}}$ _____

54. $\sqrt{32m^{13}}$ _____   **55.** $\sqrt{108(x+1)^{12}}$ _____   **56.** $\sqrt{125x^5y^2}$ _____

57. $\sqrt{y^{11}}$ _____   **58.** $\sqrt{(a+b)^5}$ _____   **59.** $\sqrt{64m^3}$ _____

60. $\sqrt{27a^3b^3}$ _____   **61.** $\sqrt{12(x+4)^9}$ _____   **62.** $\sqrt{x^7y^{12}}$ _____

Assume all variables are nonnegative.

11-4   Multiply and simplify.

1. $\sqrt{5}\sqrt{11}$ _____

2. $\sqrt{16}\sqrt{14}$ _____

3. $\sqrt{a}\sqrt{5}$ _____

4. $\sqrt{3}\sqrt{2x+5}$ _____

5. $\sqrt{x}\sqrt{x+2}$ _____

6. $\sqrt{0.5}\sqrt{3}$ _____

7. $\sqrt{3+a}\sqrt{3-a}$ _____

8. $\sqrt{x-3}\sqrt{x+4}$ _____

9. $\sqrt{2x+3}\sqrt{x+1}$ _____

10. $\sqrt{3}\sqrt{21}$ _____

11. $\sqrt{12}\sqrt{14}$ _____

12. $\sqrt{10x^2y}\sqrt{5xy}$ _____

13. $\sqrt{6a}\sqrt{30b}$ _____

14. $\sqrt{45x}\sqrt{3x}$ _____

15. $\sqrt{3x^3}\sqrt{6x}$ _____

16. $\sqrt{3a}\sqrt{15a}$ _____

17. $\sqrt{az}\sqrt{bz}$ _____

18. $\sqrt{24m^3n}\sqrt{6m^2n^2}$ _____

11-5   Simplify.

19. $\sqrt{\dfrac{1}{100}}$ _____

20. $\sqrt{\dfrac{36}{100}}$ _____

21. $\sqrt{\dfrac{500}{720}}$ _____

22. $-\sqrt{\dfrac{49}{64}}$ _____

23. $\sqrt{\dfrac{20}{405}}$ _____

24. $\sqrt{\dfrac{27}{48}}$ _____

25. $\sqrt{\dfrac{18x^2}{2}}$ _____

26. $\sqrt{\dfrac{64}{t^2}}$ _____

Divide and simplify.

27. $\dfrac{\sqrt{28}}{\sqrt{7}}$ _____

28. $\dfrac{\sqrt{108}}{\sqrt{12}}$ _____

29. $\dfrac{\sqrt{3}}{\sqrt{108}}$ _____

30. $\dfrac{\sqrt{54}}{\sqrt{150}}$ _____

31. $\dfrac{\sqrt{75x}}{\sqrt{3x}}$ _____

32. $\dfrac{\sqrt{72x^7}}{\sqrt{2x}}$ _____

33. $\dfrac{\sqrt{32x^5}}{\sqrt{8x^2}}$ _____

34. $\dfrac{\sqrt{132x^4}}{\sqrt{11x^2}}$ _____

Simplify.

35. $\sqrt{\dfrac{1}{6}}$ _____

36. $\sqrt{\dfrac{3}{7}}$ _____

37. $\sqrt{\dfrac{5}{12}}$ _____

38. $\sqrt{\dfrac{7}{18}}$ _____

39. $\sqrt{\dfrac{12}{5}}$ _____

40. $\sqrt{\dfrac{5}{x}}$ _____

41. $\sqrt{\dfrac{3x}{5}}$ _____

42. $\sqrt{\dfrac{x^2}{28}}$ _____

43. $\dfrac{\sqrt{3}}{\sqrt{8}}$ _____

44. $\dfrac{\sqrt{3}}{\sqrt{10}}$ _____

45. $\dfrac{\sqrt{15}}{\sqrt{2}}$ _____

46. $\dfrac{\sqrt{y^3}}{\sqrt{8}}$ _____

47. $\dfrac{\sqrt{6}}{\sqrt{3}}$ _____

48. $\dfrac{\sqrt{m^3n}}{\sqrt{n}}$ _____

49. $\dfrac{\sqrt{10a}}{\sqrt{12a}}$ _____

50. $\dfrac{\sqrt{y^5}}{\sqrt{xy}}$ _____

11-6   Add or subtract.

1. $11\sqrt{3} + 4\sqrt{3}$ _____

2. $-2\sqrt{x} + 4\sqrt{x}$ _____

3. $\sqrt{32} - \sqrt{18}$ _____

4. $\sqrt{48x} + \sqrt{75x^3}$ _____

5. $6\sqrt{x^2y} - \sqrt{64y}$ _____

6. $\sqrt{7} - 2\sqrt{\dfrac{1}{7}}$ _____

7. $\sqrt{\dfrac{1}{3}} + \sqrt{\dfrac{1}{12}}$ _____

8. $-12\sqrt{8} + 7\sqrt{18} + 2\sqrt{50}$ _____

9. $3\sqrt{24} + 2\sqrt{54} - 2\sqrt{27}$ _____

10. $\sqrt{16x + 32} + \sqrt{4x + 8}$ _____

11. $2a\sqrt{a^3b} + a\sqrt{ab^3} + b\sqrt{a^3b}$ _____

12. $\sqrt{36a} + 3\sqrt{4a}$ _____

11-7   Find the length of the side not given for a right triangle with hypotenuse c and legs a and b.

13. $a = 16,\ b = 30,\ c =$ _____

14. $a = 15,\ c = 25,\ b =$ _____

15. $a = 5,\ c = 13,\ b =$ _____

16. $b = 12,\ c = 20,\ a =$ _____

17. $b = 24,\ c = 25,\ a =$ _____

18. $a = 9,\ b = 12,\ c =$ _____

19. $a = 6,\ b = 8,\ c =$ _____

20. $a = 6.5,\ c = 10.5,\ b =$ _____

11-8   Solve.

21. Littleton airport is 50 miles due south of Milford. Milford is 120 miles due east of Fielding airport. How far is it from Fielding airport to Littleton airport?

_____

22. A 13-ft ladder is leaning against a building. The bottom of the ladder is 5 ft from the building. How high is the top of the ladder?

_____

11-9   Solve.

23. $\sqrt{x} = 11$ _____

24. $\sqrt{x} = 8.6$ _____

25. $12 - 6\sqrt{9n} = 0$ _____

26. $\sqrt{y + 1} + 4 = 0$ _____

27. $\sqrt{t + 1} - 4 = 9$ _____

28. $\sqrt{2x + 2} = \sqrt{x + 7}$ _____

29. $\sqrt{13 - 6x} = \sqrt{15 - 5x}$ _____

30. $\sqrt{4x + 3} = 4\sqrt{x}$ _____

31. $2\sqrt{9x} - 7 = 5$ _____

32. $\sqrt{5x - 3} = \sqrt{x + 5}$ _____

12-1   Find the indicated outputs for these functions.

1. $f(x) = x^2 - 9$; find $f(3)$, $f(0)$, $f(-2)$, $f(-5)$ _____

2. $g(x) = 3x + 1$; find $g(2)$, $g(-8)$, $g(-1)$, $g(0)$ _____

3. $h(t) = |t| - 2$; find $h(-1)$, $h(3)$, $h(0)$, $h(2)$ _____

4. $k(x) = x^3 - 2x$; find $k(-3)$, $k(2)$, $k(0)$, $k(-1)$ _____

12-2   Graph each function.

5. $f(x) = 2x - 1$, where the domain is $\{-3, -1, 0, 2, 3\}$

6. $g(x) = -2x + 3$

7. $h(x) = |x| - 2$

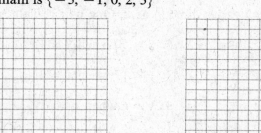
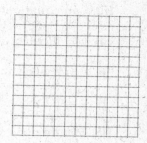

12-3   Write a linear function describing each situation and solve.

8. Travis rented a typewriter for $15.00 plus $1.65 per day. Find the cost if he kept the typewriter for 12 days.

_____

9. Robert earned $4.50 an hour for painting a garage, plus a bonus of $10.00. He worked for 6 hours. How much did he earn?

_____

10. Ryla bought 14 yards of carpet for $13.50 per yard, plus a cutting fee of $35. What was the total cost of the carpet?

_____

11. On Friday, Alanna earned $5.10 per hour, plus $82.00 in tips. If she worked 8 hours, how much did she earn?

_____

12. A mail-order company sells dried apples for $4.50 per pound, plus $2.25 for shipping and handling. Find the cost of five pounds of fruit.

_____

12-4   Graph each function.

1. $f(x) = \frac{1}{2} x^2$

2. $f(x) = x^2 - 5$

3. $f(x) = -x^2 + 3$

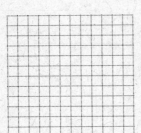

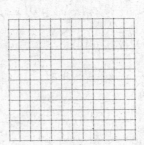

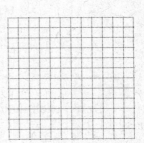

12-5   Find an equation of variation where y varies directly as x. One pair of values is given.

4. $y = 12$ when $x = 20$ _____

5. $y = 50$ when $x = 150$ _____

6. $y = 9$ when $x = 3$ _____

7. $y = 17$ when $x = 3$ _____

8. $y = 1.2$ when $x = 4$ _____

9. $y = 6$ when $x = 1.5$ _____

10. The number of pages Mara can read varies directly
with time. She can read 15 pages in 20 minutes.
How many pages can she read in 50 minutes?   _____

12-6   Find an equation of variation where y varies inversely as x. One pair of values is given.

11. $y = 9$ when $x = 3$ _____

12. $y = 0.5$ when $x = 6$ _____

13. $y = 4$ when $x = 8$ _____

14. $y = 14$ when $x = 10$ _____

15. $y = 8$ when $x = 0.25$ _____

16. $y = 0.3$ when $x = 0.5$ _____

17. The time it takes to set up tables for a banquet
dinner varies inversely as the number of people
setting tables. It takes two hours for four people to
set up the tables. How long will it take six people
to do the job?   _____

12-7   Find an equation of joint variation for each. Then solve for the missing value.

18. x varies jointly as y and z. One set of values is
$x = 42$, $y = 3$, $z = 7$. Find x when $y = 11$ and $z = 3$.   _____

19. a varies directly as b and inversely as c. One set of
values is $a = 6$, $b = 9$, and $c = 3$. Find a when
$b = 10$ and $c = 4$.   _____

SKILLS PRACTICE 35

For use with Lessons 13-1–13-3

NAME _____

DATE _____

13-1   Write each equation in standard form and determine a, b, and c.

1. $5x - 4 = x^2 + 2$ _____

2. $5x^2 = 16$ _____

3. $2x^2 - 17 = 5x$ _____

4. $35 = x^2 - 10x$ _____

Solve.

5. $x^2 + 2x - 35 = 0$ _____

6. $3x^2 - 15x = 0$ _____

7. $x^2 - 11x + 24 = 0$ _____

8. $2x^2 + 9x - 5 = 0$ _____

9. $x^2 + 5x - 36 = 0$ _____

10. $2x^2 - 11x + 12 = 0$ _____

11. $3x^2 - x - 10 = 0$ _____

12. $6y^2 - 13y + 6 = 0$ _____

13-2   Solve.

13. $x^2 = 5$ _____

14. $4x^2 = 48$ _____

15. $8x^2 = 36$ _____

16. $(x - 3)^2 = 16$ _____

17. $(x - 9)^2 = 10$ _____

18. $(x + 4)^2 = 15$ _____

19. $2x^2 - 30x = 0$ _____

20. $6x^2 + 15x = 0$ _____

21. $5x^2 - 45 = 0$ _____

22. $8x^2 - 10x = 0$ _____

23. $x^2 + 8x + 16 = 25$ _____

24. $16y^2 + 25 = 25$ _____

25. $x^2 - 4x + 4 = 16$ _____

26. $x^2 + 10x + 25 = 33$ _____

13-3   Complete the square.

27. $y^2 - 3y$ _____

28. $m^2 - 4m$ _____

29. $t^2 + 7t$ _____

30. $x^2 - 14x$ _____

31. $x^2 - 9x$ _____

32. $y^2 + 16y$ _____

Solve by completing the square.

33. $x^2 - 6x - 20 = 0$ _____

34. $x^2 - 8x + 10 = 0$ _____

35. $t^2 + 8t - 5 = 0$ _____

36. $m^2 + 6m - 4 = 0$ _____

37. $2x^2 - 8x + 7 = 0$ _____

38. $y^2 - 4y - 1 = 0$ _____

39. $x^2 + 10x + 12 = 0$ _____

40. $3y^2 - 2y - 1 = 0$ _____

41. $4x^2 - 12x + 5 = 0$ _____

42. $2m^2 + 4m - 9 = 0$ _____

43. $x^2 - 12x + 9 = 0$ _____

44. $3x^2 - 8x + 1 = 0$ _____

13-4 Solve using the quadratic formula.

1. $x^2 + 4x - 45 = 0$ _____

2. $2x^2 - x - 21 = 0$ _____

3. $x^2 - 49 = 0$ _____

4. $x^2 + 8x + 16 = 5$ _____

5. $x^2 - 3x - 2 = 0$ _____

6. $2x^2 - 10x + 9 = 0$ _____

7. $x^2 + 2x + 10 = 0$ _____

8. $3x^2 + 12x + 8 = 0$ _____

9. $x^2 - 3x - 5 = 0$ _____

10. $5x^2 = 6 + 2x$ _____

11. $4x^2 - 5x + 1 = 0$ _____

12. $7x^2 = 3$ _____

13-5 Solve each rational equation.

13. $x + \dfrac{3}{x} = 4$ _____

14. $x - 4 = \dfrac{6}{x - 4}$ _____

15. $\dfrac{x^2}{x - 7} - \dfrac{2}{x - 7} = 0$ _____

16. $\dfrac{-5}{x} - \dfrac{2}{x + 4} = 1$ _____

17. $\dfrac{3}{x + 4} + \dfrac{7}{x - 4} = 2$ _____

18. $\dfrac{15}{x + 3} - \dfrac{1}{x^2 - 9} = 2$ _____

19. $x - 5 = \dfrac{9}{x - 5}$ _____

20. $\dfrac{12}{x + 3} + \dfrac{2}{x - 3} = 2$ _____

13-6 Solve each radical equation.

21. $\sqrt{6 + x} = x + 4$ _____

22. $\sqrt{x - 8} = x - 10$ _____

23. $x - 1 = \sqrt{5x + 1}$ _____

24. $\sqrt{60 - 7x} = 6 - x$ _____

25. $2\sqrt{3x + 1} = x + 3$ _____

26. $\sqrt{x^2 + 11} = x + 1$ _____

27. $\sqrt{x + 2} = x - 4$ _____

28. $\sqrt{x^2 + 15} = x + 1$ _____

13-7 Solve.

29. The width of a rectangle is half the length. The area is 40.5 cm². Find the length and the width.

_____

30. The hypotenuse of a right triangle is 20 cm long. One leg is 4 cm longer than the other. Find the length of the legs.

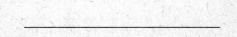

31. A picture frame is 12 cm by 8 cm. There are 60 cm² of picture showing. Find the width of the frame.

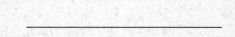

Mixed Review Worksheets

The following 26 blackline masters are worksheets for extra practice in a mixed-review format. Every worksheet provides practice from a variety of lessons in the student text. The appropriate time to give each worksheet is indicated at the top of the sheets. The lesson that each group of exercises has been modeled after is indicated in the left margin.

You will find these worksheets helpful for reviewing and reinforcing concepts with all of your students. These worksheets could also be incorporated within the context of a cumulative or semester review.

MIXED REVIEW 1

For use after Lesson 1-4

NAME _____

DATE _____

Evaluate each expression.

1-1

1. $x - 9$ for $x = 23$ _____

2. $7(3 + b)$ for $b = 4$ _____

3. $5 + c + c$ for $c = 2$ _____

4. $m - n$ for $m = 63$ and $n = 45$ _____

1-3

5. $2m^2$ for $m = 7$ _____

6. $(2w)^2$ for $w = 6$ _____

7. $(3c)^4$ for $c = 0$ _____

8. $3s^4$ for $s = 2$ _____

9. $4a^2$ for $a = 7$ _____

10. $(4t)^2$ for $t = 5$ _____

1-4

11. $3y^3 - 16$ for $y = 4$ _____

12. $(a + 2)^4$ for $a = 1$ _____

13. $4(n - 3)$ for $n = 7$ _____

14. $(a + 3) \cdot (5 - a)$ for $a = 4$ _____

15. $\dfrac{8 + 3a}{7a}$ for $a = 2$ _____

16. $\dfrac{w^2 + w}{6w}$ for $w = 3$ _____

Simplify.

1-1

17. $9 \div 3 + 7$ _____

18. $52 \div 13 + 3$ _____

19. $25 \times 2 \div 5 - 9$ _____

20. $10 - 6 \times 6 \times 0$ _____

1-2

21. $\dfrac{m}{5m}$ _____

22. $\dfrac{16}{8}$ _____

23. $\dfrac{36c}{16}$ _____

24. $\dfrac{3ab}{27ab}$ _____

25. $\dfrac{21x}{49y}$ _____

26. $\dfrac{6r}{7rs}$ _____

27. $\dfrac{10cd}{c}$ _____

28. $\dfrac{12bt}{20ct}$ _____

29. $\dfrac{7wz}{21zt}$ _____

1-4

Calculate.

30. $5 + 2^2$ _____

31. $(5 + 2)^2$ _____

32. $5 \cdot 2^2$ _____

33. $(5 - 2)^2$ _____

34. $5 - 2^2$ _____

35. $(5 - 4)^8$ _____

1-3

Write using exponential notation.

36. $3 \cdot 3 \cdot 3 \cdot 3 \cdot 3$ _____

37. $27 \cdot m \cdot m \cdot m$ _____

38. $s \cdot s \cdot s \cdot s \cdot s \cdot s$ _____

39. $2 \cdot t \cdot t \cdot t \cdot t$ _____

Write an equivalent expression.

1-2

40. $2y + 5$ _____

41. $6 \cdot w$ _____

1-4

42. $(a + b) + 1$ _____

43. $2 \cdot (m \cdot n)$ _____

44. $(x \cdot y) \cdot 4$ _____

45. $12 + (s + t)$ _____

Write an equivalent expression.

1-4

1. $(m + n) + 13$ _____

2. $6 \cdot (a \cdot b)$ _____

1-5

3. $7(x + y)$ _____

4. $(4 + s)t$ _____

5. $6(2a + 1)$ _____

6. $5(c + 3 + 2w)$ _____

1-6

Write as an algebraic expression.

7. t divided among s _____

8. r more than p _____

9. the sum of x and y _____

10. the product of u and v _____

11. Mike sold H hats. Nate sold three times as many hats as Mike. Write an expression for the number of hats Nate sold.

_____

12. Together, Sala and Terry saved $10.00. Sala saved D dollars. Write an expression for the amount Terry saved.

_____

1-5

Factor and check by multiplying.

13. $6x + 21y$ _____

14. $6a + 24b$ _____

15. $12m + 3n$ _____

16. $4 + 6w + 8z$ _____

1-5

Collect like terms.

17. $11a + 5 + a$ _____

18. $6s + 13 + 2s + t$ _____

19. $m^2 + 4m + 2m^2$ _____

20. $u^2 + w + 3u^2 + w^2$ _____

21. $3a + 4b + 2b + c$ _____

22. $9 + 7c + 2c + 11$ _____

1-7

Each pair of equations is equivalent. Tell what was done to the first equation to get the second equation.

23. $2x - 11 = 5$
$2x - 1 = 15$ _____

24. $18x = 48$
$3x = 8$ _____

Solve mentally.

25. $5m = 100$ _____

26. $w - 35 = 35$ _____

27. $\frac{s}{7} = 2$ _____

1-3

Evaluate each expression.

28. $3t^3$ for $t = 3$ _____

29. $(2t)^2$ for $t = 4$ _____

30. x^4 for $x = 2$ _____

Evaluate for $a = 10$, $b = 2$, $c = 3$.

1-1

1. $15a$ _____ **2.** $a - c$ _____ **3.** $(b + 11) - 6$ _____

4. $\dfrac{a}{5b}$ _____ **5.** $\dfrac{ac}{b}$ _____ **6.** $\dfrac{(a + 5)}{c}$ _____

1-3

7. $c^2 + 2$ _____ **8.** $b^3 - 1$ _____ **9.** a^1 _____

10. $(2c)^3$ _____ **11.** $5b^4$ _____ **12.** $(3a)^2$ _____

1-5

Collect like terms.

13. $3x - 9y - x - x + y$ _____ **14.** $6n^2 - 3n - 2n^2 + 5n$ _____

15. $14c - 11a + a - 5$ _____ **16.** $-6 + y - 3y^2 + 11 - 2y$ _____

2-3

Add.

17. $16 + (-19) + 30 + (-27) + 4 + 37 + (-108)$ _____

18. $-19 + 63 + (-24)$ _____ **19.** $4.2 + (-1.7) + 3.9 + (-0.4)$ _____

Simplify.

1-2

20. $\dfrac{16xy}{96y}$ _____ **21.** $\dfrac{5t}{30}$ _____ **22.** $\dfrac{17ab}{5bc}$ _____

1-1

23. $16 \div 4 + 7$ _____ **24.** $6 \times 4 - 7 \times 3$ _____

25. $15 + 3 \times 5$ _____ **26.** $41 - 9 \times 4$ _____

2-4

27. $11 - (-3) + 35 + (-1)$ _____ **28.** $3x - (5x) + (-2x) - x$ _____

29. $-64 + 19 - 3 - (-11)$ _____ **30.** $14 - 18 + (-25) - (-40)$ _____

31. $7a - 2b + 21 - a + 5b$ _____ **32.** $15y - 2y + y^2 + 3y$ _____

2-1

Write a true sentence using $<$ or $>$.

33. -1 _____ -4 **34.** $|6|$ _____ $|3|$ **35.** $|-4|$ _____ $|2|$ **36.** -3 _____ -2

2-3

Find the additive inverse of each.

37. 1.75 _____ **38.** -19 _____ **39.** -1.04 _____ **40.** 4 _____

1-5

Factor and check.

41. $14a + 28b + 35$ _____ **42.** $12 + 30a + 78c$ _____

43. $350x + 90y$ _____ **44.** $ax + ay + az$ _____

NAME _____

DATE _____

Evaluate.

1-4

1. $t + 5^2$ for $t = 3$ _____

2. $(t + 5)^2$ for $t = 3$ _____

3. $a(4 + a)$ for $a = 2$ _____

4. $(m + 2)(m - 7)$ for $m = 9$ _____

5. $\dfrac{2n + 1}{3n}$ for $n = 7$ _____

6. $\dfrac{c^2 + c}{4c}$ for $c = 3$ _____

1-9

7. $A = lw$ for $l = 12.5$ ft and $w = 18$ in. (an area formula) _____

8. $P = 2g + f$ for $g = 53$ and $f = 11$ (a sports formula) _____

9. $t = \dfrac{D}{r}$ for $D = 375$ m and $r = 50$ m/s (a time formula) _____

2-6

Find the reciprocal.

10. 0.75 _____

11. $1\dfrac{1}{2}$ _____

12. $-3c$ _____

13. $\dfrac{-2m}{n}$ _____

2-7

Collect like terms.

14. $9a - 7b + 5a$ _____

15. $6x - 14x$ _____

16. $6y + 9y - y$ _____

17. $\dfrac{1}{3}w + \dfrac{2}{3}z - \dfrac{1}{3}w + \dfrac{2}{3}z$ _____

18. $3m - 1.2n + 2.5n - m$ _____

2-7

Factor.

19. $9x + 36y$ _____

20. $5x - 30 + 15y$ _____

21. $\dfrac{1}{2}a - \dfrac{1}{4}b$ _____

Multiply or divide.

2-5

22. $-2(-5)(3)$ _____

23. $4(5)(-2)$ _____

24. $(-9)(-1)(-3)$ _____

2-6

25. $\left(\dfrac{-1}{2}\right)\left(\dfrac{-1}{3}\right)\left(\dfrac{2}{5}\right)$ _____

26. $\left(\dfrac{3}{4}\right) \div \left(\dfrac{-1}{2}\right)$ _____

27. $\left(\dfrac{-1}{2}\right) \cdot \left(\dfrac{-8}{3}\right)$ _____

28. $\dfrac{3}{4} \div \left(\dfrac{-5}{8}\right)$ _____

29. $\dfrac{-5}{6} \div \dfrac{3}{2}$ _____

30. $\dfrac{7}{10} \div \dfrac{3}{4}$ _____

2-3

Solve.

31. On Friday Stephanie worked as a waitress. She was paid $40. She spent $23 on a pair of shoes, lent her brother $16.50, earned $9.25 in tips, and paid $6 to go to the movies. How much did she have left? _____

MIXED REVIEW 5

For use after Lesson 3-4

NAME _____

DATE _____

1-9   Evaluate.

1. $A = \frac{1}{2}bh$ for $b = 14$ ft and $h = 10$ ft (an area formula) _____

2. $P = 2l + 2w$ for $l = 815$ cm and $w = 7.0$ m (a perimeter formula) _____

3. $D = rt$ for $r = 55$ mi/h and $t = 8.75$ h (a distance formula) _____

Simplify.

2-8   4. $5y - (4x - 2y) - 2(x + 2y)$ _____ 5. $(-5y + 4x) - (-3x + y)$ _____

3-1   6. $-11 + t = 14$ _____ 7. $m + 51 = 12$ _____ 8. $r + (-2) = -6$ _____

3-2   9. $-c = 6$ _____ 10. $-3t = 54$ _____ 11. $\frac{2m}{5} = 4$ _____

3-3   12. $9s - 11 = 16$ _____ 13. $3c - 8c = 20$ _____

14. $4(3y - 1) - 5y = 17$ _____ 15. $-7m + 2(5m + 1) = 6$ _____

2-2   Use either $>$ or $<$ to write a true sentence.

16. 1.75 _____ 1.57 17. -3.8 _____ -3.9 18. 1.016 _____ 1.061

19. 0.001 _____ 0.0011 20. -4.572 _____ -4.275 21. -0.043 _____ -0.403

2-4   Simplify.

22. $16 - (-4) - 9 + (-2)$ _____ 23. $8 - 1 - 15 - 4 - (-21)$ _____

24. $-3 - (-7) + (-6) - 2$ _____ 25. $-5 + (-1) - 7 - (-19) - 6$ _____

Write an equation that can be used to solve the problem.

2-9   26. An adult's ticket for the train costs $2.50 more than a child's ticket. An adult's ticket costs $7.50. How much does a child's ticket cost? _____

3-1   27. A number increased by 9 is -2. Find the number. _____

3-2   28. A number multiplied by 16 is -112. Find the number. _____

29. Theo paid the same price for each of 6 tickets to the football game. He paid a total of $108. What was the price of each ticket? _____

3-4   30. Today Kerry read seven less than twice the number of pages she read yesterday. If she read a total of 122 pages, how many pages did she read yesterday? _____

MIXED REVIEW 6

For use after Lesson 3-9

NAME _____

DATE _____

2-1   Write a true sentence using either $<$ or $>$.

1. 9 _____ $5\frac{1}{2}$ **2.** 1.04 _____ 1.40 **3.** $|3|$ _____ $|-7|$ **4.** $|2.16|$ ____ $|2.161|$

5. $|10|$ _____ $|8|$ **6.** -1.23 __ -1.32 **7.** 6.29 _____ 6.30 **8.** $|0.01|$ __ $|-0.02|$

2-6   Find the reciprocal.

9. $5\frac{1}{2}$ _____   **10.** $\frac{107}{40}$ _____   **11.** -0.5 _____   **12.** $\frac{-a}{b}$ _____

13. $7y$ _____   **14.** $\frac{-1}{2n}$ _____   **15.** -6 _____   **16.** 1.75 _____

2-7   Factor.

17. $9x - 18y + 9$ _____   **18.** $4s + 16t$ _____   **19.** $49 - 14x$ _____

1-7   Solve for the given replacement set.

20. $\frac{1}{2}x^2 - x + 1 = 5$ $\{2, 4, 6\}$ _____   **21.** $y - 15 + y^3 = 100$ $\{1, 3, 5\}$ _____

Solve.

3-9   **22.** $\frac{x}{8} = \frac{3}{16}$ _____   **23.** $\frac{9}{5} = \frac{63}{x}$ _____   **24.** $\frac{24}{x} = \frac{18}{4}$ _____

25. Out of 300 students in the junior class 75 play sports. In a typical classroom of 40 students, how many play sports?

_____

26. At a pen factory, 3 out of every 80 pens are defective. If the factory produces 7680 pens in a day, how many will be defective?

_____

3-2   **27.** $-\frac{m}{7} = 5$ _____   **28.** $\frac{3}{5}r = 42$ _____   **29.** $\frac{5}{8}t = 10$ _____

3-5   **30.** $6n - (2n + 4) = 16$ _____   **31.** $2(t + 5) - 10 = 14$ _____

3-6   **32.** $\frac{3}{5}x + 2x + \frac{2}{5}x = 2x + 5$ _____   **33.** $\frac{2}{3}t - 1 = \frac{t}{2}$ _____

3-8   **34.** $\frac{|t|}{6} = 6$ _____   **35.** $3|a| = 84$ _____   **36.** $|m| = 0$ _____

37. $5|k| - 2 = 33$ _____   **38.** $|-3| + |x| = 5$ _____   **39.** $-2|b| = -12$ _____

3-2   **40.** A box of eighteen notebooks costs $28.62. What is the cost of a single notebook?

_____

41. Abel's Bakery produces 152 loaves of bread each day. These are 38% of the total loaves produced. How many loaves does the bakery produce each day? _____

52

MIXED REVIEW 7

For use after Lesson 4-2

NAME _____

DATE _____

1-4   Use an associative property to write an equivalent expression.

1. $(5 \cdot a) \cdot 7$ _____   **2.** $m + (n + 1)$ _____   **3.** $(a + b) + c$ _____

1-5   Use the distributive property to write an equivalent expression.

4. $2(3w + 2x)$ _____   **5.** $3(5x + 3y + 2)$ _____   **6.** $7(a + 3b + c)$ _____

Simplify.

2-4   **7.** $5 - (-8x) - 3 - x$ _____   **8.** $-3 - 2 - (-7)$ _____

9. $1.4 - 1.8 - (-3)$ _____   **10.** $3y - (-2y) - 3y$ _____

2-8   **11.** $7a - (5a - 4)$ _____   **12.** $3a - 2b - 2(2a - b)$ _____

13. $[2(3y + 1) + 5] - 5y$ _____   **14.** $5[9 - 2(3x + 4)]$ _____

3-4   Write as an algebraic expression.

15. The product of two consecutive integers _____

16. The sum of three consecutive even integers _____

17. Seven times the sum of a number and 5 _____

Solve.

3-5   **18.** $6x - 24 = -48$ _____   **19.** $-5t = 81 + 4t$ _____

20. $-10a - 6a = 48$ _____   **21.** $2 - 3x = -4x + 16$ _____

3-8   **22.** $|-3| + |-7| + |c| = 10$ _____   **23.** $|a| - 21 = 15$ _____

24. $2|y| + 10 = 38$ _____   **25.** $3|m| - 5 = 10$ _____

3-9   **26.** Cory works 6 hours to earn $27. How many hours must he work to earn $72? _____

4-2   Solve and graph.

27. $x - 3 > 1$ _____

28. $2x + 1 > -5$ _____

29. $3y - 4 - y < -4$ _____

Evaluate for $x = 8$ and $y = 6$.

1-1

1. $\dfrac{(x + 4)}{y}$ _____

2. $xy - 10$ _____

3. $3x - 4y$ _____

4. $\dfrac{xy}{16}$ _____

1-3

5. x^3 _____

6. $y^2 + 9$ _____

7. $2x^2$ _____

8. $(2y)^2$ _____

Multiply.

2-5

9. $(-7)(-3)$ _____

10. $6(-4)0$ _____

11. $(-2)(-3)(-4)$ _____

2-7

12. $(5.5)(4.2)$ _____

13. $-3(18)$ _____

14. $(-1)(1)(-1)(1)$ _____

Give the number property that justifies each statement.

1-4

15. $3 \cdot (a \cdot b) = (3 \cdot a) \cdot b$ _____

1-5

16. $5(a + b + c) = 5a + 5b + 5c$ _____

1-4

17. $r + (s + t) = (r + s) + t$ _____

1-5

Collect like terms.

18. $2y^2 + 7w + 8y^2 + w + w + y^2$ _____

19. $36 + 27c + 25 + 4c + 9 + c + 1$ _____

20. $1.2x + 3.8 + 5.77x + 3.05 + 4 + 8.1x$ _____

Solve.

3-11

21. The sum of four consecutive integers is 210. What are
the integers? _____

22. The sum of Gino's weight and Larry's weight is 287.
Gino weighs 17 pounds less than Larry. How much
does Gino weigh? How much does Larry weigh? _____

4-3

23. $16x \leq 8$ _____

24. $7m > -21$ _____

25. $-2c < 26$ _____

26. $-5a \geq -110$ _____

4-4

27. $5 + 3x > 17$ _____

28. $7 - 2y < 19$ _____

29. $6 - 2a - 5a > -36$ _____

30. $10 - 3y < 5y - 70$ _____

MIXED REVIEW 9

For use after Lesson 5-4

NAME _____

DATE _____

Give the number property that justifies each statement.

1-4   **1.** $(4 \cdot a) \cdot b = 4 \cdot (a \cdot b)$ _____

1-5   **2.** $3(2m + 5n) = 6m + 15n$ _____

1-4   **3.** $(x + y) + z = x + (y + z)$ _____

1-2   **4.** $xy = yx$ _____

1-2   **5.** $m \cdot 1 = m$ _____

Use $<$ or $>$ to write a true sentence.

2-1   **6.** -3 ____ -4 **7.** 2 ____ -3 **8.** -1 ____ 6

2-2   **9.** -2.5 ____ -3.1 **10.** -1.7 ____ -1.27 **11.** 1.06 ____ 1.6

       12. $\dfrac{3}{8}$ ____ $\dfrac{3}{7}$ **13.** $\dfrac{-1}{2}$ ____ $\dfrac{-1}{4}$ **14.** $\dfrac{5}{2}$ ____ $\dfrac{5}{7}$

2-7   Factor.

       15. $17m + 68$ _____   **16.** $-8a + 12$ _____

       17. $18y + 24$ _____   **18.** $4a + 20b - 16$ _____

2-8   Remove parentheses and simplify.

       19. $-5(m + 6) + 12$ _____   **20.** $17 - 3(9 - 2a)$ _____

       21. $3y + 2(6 - 5y)$ _____   **22.** $-5m + 7(2m - 3)$ _____

       Solve.

3-1   **23.** $2\dfrac{1}{5} - y = \dfrac{3}{2}$ _____   **24.** $m - \dfrac{3}{8} = 2\dfrac{1}{2}$ _____

3-2   **25.** $1.2a = -1.44$ _____   **26.** $-\left(\dfrac{3}{2}\right)c = \dfrac{18}{4}$ _____

3-3   **27.** $2(9x + 5) = 46$ _____   **28.** $9 = 3(5 - 2t)$ _____

5-2   Simplify.

       29. $(2x^5y^2)^3$ _____   **30.** $\left(\dfrac{a^4}{b^2}\right)^3$ _____

5-4   Write using scientific notation.

       31. 0.0034 _____   **32.** 34000000 _____

55

MIXED REVIEW 10

For use after Lesson 5-9

1-6   Write as an algebraic expression.

1. seven more than t _____

2. half the sum of m and n _____

3. m divided among 4 _____

4. the product of x and y _____

Multiply or divide.

2-5

5. $(-3)(2)(-7)$ _____

6. $4 \cdot (-1)(-1)$ _____

7. $6(2)(-3)$ _____

8. $\left(\dfrac{-1}{2}\right)\left(\dfrac{3}{8}\right)$ _____

9. $\left(\dfrac{-2}{3}\right)\left(\dfrac{-1}{5}\right)$ _____

10. $\dfrac{-5}{9}\left(\dfrac{1}{3}\right)\left(\dfrac{-1}{3}\right)$ _____

5-3

11. $(4y)(-2y)$ _____

12. $(3a^2b)(2b)$ _____

13. $(5mn)(-2m^2)$ _____

2-6

14. $\dfrac{-12.1}{11}$ _____

15. $\dfrac{125}{-50}$ _____

16. $\dfrac{-16}{-120}$ _____

5-3

17. $\dfrac{y^5}{y^2}$ _____

18. $\dfrac{-20a^2}{5a}$ _____

19. $\dfrac{12m^2n}{3mn}$ _____

2-8   Collect like terms.

20. $6m - 4.2m + 1.3n + 1.07m - 2n - 1.15n$ _____

21. $-4a + c + 9c - 15c + 11a - c - c - 7c$ _____

Solve.

3-8

22. $|a| = 14$ _____

23. $5|x| = 65$ _____

24. $2|y| = 7$ _____

4-3

25. $15n \le 60$ _____

26. $8c > -104$ _____

27 $-3y > 48$ _____

4-4

28. $6 + 5y < -14$ _____

29. $3 - 4m < -9$ _____

30. $7 + 4c > -2 + c$ _____

Simplify.

2-8

31. $-4y + (-y) + 11y$ _____

32. $8x - 4(2 - 3x) + 6$ _____

33. $5 - 7(m + 2)$ _____

34. $-2m - 9(m + 4) - 7$ _____

5-2

35. $(12m^2n)^2$ _____

36. $(3a^2)^3$ _____

37. $(-2x^5y)^3$ _____

5-7

38. $(3x^5 + 5x^3 - 2x^2 + 9) + (-2x^3 + 3x^4 - 9x + 19)$ _____

39. $(4x^5 + 9x^4 - 8x^2 + x + 1) + (3x^4 + 8x^2 - x - 2)$ _____

5-9   Multiply.

40. $(5x - 7)(3x + 2)$ _____

41. $(2x + 3y)(3x - 2y)$ _____

56

Simplify.

1-1

1. $24 \div (2 \cdot 4) - 1$ _____

2. $(57 - 8) \div 7 - 2$ _____

2-4

3. $6 - 2x - (-3x) - 1$ _____

4. $4x - 1 - (-2x) - 9x$ _____

2-8

5. $-5(2x + 1) - 9$ _____

6. $26 - 3(x + 5) - 7x$ _____

5-1

7. $y^7 \cdot y^5$ _____

8. $m^3 \cdot m^4 \cdot m$ _____

9. $(a^2c)(a^5c^2)$ _____

10. $\dfrac{a^{13}}{a^7}$ _____

11. $\dfrac{x^3y^5}{xy^4}$ _____

12. $\dfrac{a^5b^2c^3}{abc^2}$ _____

5-2

13. $(5x^3y^2)^2$ _____

14. $(2a^5b^3)^4$ _____

15. $(-5m^3n)^2$ _____

Multiply.

2-5

16. $4(-3)(-7)$ _____

17. $6(-1)(-1)(1)$ _____

18. $-2(-9)(3)(4)$ _____

2-7

19. $6(-3a - 5)$ _____

20. $-9(3c + 2)$ _____

21. $-5(-2y - 7)$ _____

5-3

22. $(4xy)(-2x^2y^5)$ _____

23. $(3a^2)(-7a)(-2a^7)$ _____

5-9

24. $2x(3x - 7)$ _____

25. $3y^2(y^2 - 11y + 6)$ _____

26. $(x + 5)(x - 2)$ _____

27. $(2a^2 + 1)(3a^2 - 4)$ _____

Evaluate for $a = 2$, $b = -3$.

1-3

28. $(2b)^2$ _____

29. $7a^4$ _____

30. $b^2 - 2$ _____

3-8

31. $|ab|$ _____

32. $-b|a|$ _____

33. $3a|b|$ _____

5-6

34. $5a + b$ _____

35. $a^2 - 2ab + 3b^2$ _____

5-5

Identify the terms. Give the coefficient of each term.

36. $7x^5 + 3x^3 - 9x^2 + x + 3$ _____

37. $-4x^3y + 7xy^5 - 19$ _____

Factor.

1-5

38. $12x + 15y + 9$ _____

39. $24m + 6n + 30$ _____

2-8

40. $9x - 27y + 12$ _____

41. $6a - 18b + 48c$ _____

6-1

42. $25x^3 - 10x^2 - 40x$ _____

43. $8m^3n^2 + 12m^2n - 20m$ _____

6-2

44. $x^4 - 25$ _____

45. $3x^2 - 243$ _____

Solve.

3-5

1. $5a + 6 - 3a = 7a - 4$ _____

2. $-9(c - 4) = 9$ _____

3. $1.2x - 5.7 = 3.1x + 3.8$ _____

4. $5y - 2(y - 9) = 6 - y$ _____

3-8

5. $|c| + 4 = 15$ _____

6. $3|m| = 162$ _____

4-4

7. $-7t \leq 45 + 2t$ _____

8. $n + 7 \geq 3(n - 1) + 2$ _____

6-8

9. $(y - 4)(y + 1) = 0$ _____

10. $m(2m + 6) = 0$ _____

11. $x^2 + 2x = 35$ _____

12. $25x^2 = 100$ _____

5-4

Write using standard notation.

13. 1.775×10^3 _____

14. 6.1×10^{-4} _____

15. 1.01×10^5 _____

Write using scientific notation.

16. 8,765,000 _____

17. 0.00671 _____

18. 31.065 _____

Multiply.

5-10

19. $(x + 13)(x - 13)$ _____

20. $(4m + 7)(4m - 7)$ _____

21. $(-3t + 2)(-3t + 2)$ _____

22. $(5c - 3)^2$ _____

5-11

23. $(2a^2 - 5a + 1)(a - 2)$ _____

24. $(5y^2 + 10y - 9)(2y + 3)$ _____

5-7

Add or subtract.

25. $(5m^3n - 4mn^3 + 2n^3) + (3m^3n + m^2n^2 - 2n^3)$ _____

26. $(3a^2 + 5ab - 7b^2) - (2a^3 + ab - 4b^2)$ _____

27. $(7x^4 + 6x^2 + x + 12) - (5x^4 + 2x^3 + 4x^2 - 5x)$ _____

Factor.

6-3

28. $t^2 + 16t + 64$ _____

29. $x^2 - 20x + 100$ _____

6-4

30. $c^2 + 4c - 21$ _____

31. $y^2 - y - 20$ _____

6-5

32. $2a^2 + 14a + 24$ _____

33. $5n^2 - 5n - 10$ _____

6-6

34. $x^3 + 4x^2 + 2x + 8$ _____

35. $3y^3 - 21y^2 + 5y - 35$ _____

6-7

36. $5a^2 - 20$ _____

37. $y^2 + y - 306$ _____

MIXED REVIEW 13

For use after Lesson 7-3

3-10   Translate to an equation and solve.

   1. What percent of 120 is 36? _____

   2. What is 12% of 60? _____

   3. 15 is what percent of 75? _____

5-6   Evaluate each polynomial for $n = -3$.

   4. $2n^2 + 5n - 3$ _____   **5.** $n(n + 1)(n - 1)$ _____

5-5   Identify the degree of each term and the degree of the polynomial.

   6. $x^5 - 6x^3 + 5x^2 - 2x - 4$ _____   **7.** $3x^3y - 11x^2y^4 + 4xy^3 - 19$ _____

   Multiply.

5-1   **8.** $2^3 \cdot 2^4 \cdot 2^5$ _____   **9.** $y \cdot y^7 \cdot y^4$ _____   **10.** $(5m)^4(5m)^6$ _____

5-3   **11.** $(4y)(17y)$ _____   **12.** $(3a)(5ab^2)$ _____   **13.** $(mn^2)(2mn)$ _____

5-9   **14.** $5c(c^2 + 2)$ _____   **15.** $2t(3t - 7)$ _____   **16.** $(x + 4)(x - 4)$ _____

   Factor.

6-2   **17.** $9x^2 - 16$ _____   **18.** $2y^4 - 162$ _____

6-3   **19.** $a^2 - 14a + 49$ _____   **20.** $48m^2 + 72m + 27$ _____

6-4   **21.** $y^2 - 10y + 21$ _____   **22.** $n^2 - n - 72$ _____

6-5   **23.** $12x^2 + 21x - 108$ _____   **24.** $7y^2 - 54y + 35$ _____

7-3   Graph, using intercepts.

   25. $3x - 4y = 12$ **26.** $2x + 3y = 6$

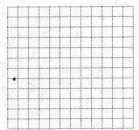   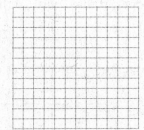

7-2   Determine whether the given point is a solution of $2x + 5y = 24$.

   27. $(2, 7)$ _____   **28.** $(-3, 6)$ _____

59

NAME _____

DATE _____

Use the distributive property to write an equivalent expression.

1-5

1. $-3(6x - 2y + 5z)$ _____

2. $8(6c + 7d + 1)$ _____

5-9

3. $-4x^3(5x^2 - 7x - 6)$ _____

4. $3a^2b(4ab - 3b + 1)$ _____

5-2

Simplify.

5. $(a^4)^3$ _____

6. $(-4x^3)^3$ _____

7. $(2xy^2)^4$ _____

6-7

Factor.

8. $a^6b^2 - a^5b^3 - a^2b^2$ _____

9. $16a^2 - 49y^2$ _____

10. $9x^2 - 60xy + 100y^2$ _____

11. $24c^2 - cd - 3d^2$ _____

3-7

Solve the formulas for the given letter.

12. $V = \pi r^2h$, for h _____

13. $E = \frac{1}{2} mv^2$, for m _____

Translate to an equation and find all solutions.

3-1

14. Celeste collected 416 aluminum cans. That was 87 more cans than Louis collected. How many cans did Louis collect?

_____

6-9

15. The square of a number is 3 less than 4 times the number. Find the number.

_____

16. The width of a rectangle is 3 cm less than the length. The area of the rectangle is 54 cm². Find the width and the length.

_____

5-5

Identify the terms. Give the coefficient and degree of each term.

17. $45x^4 - 4y^2$ _____

18. $3x^2y^2 - 5x + 9$ _____

7-4

Find the slopes, if they exist, of the lines containing these points.

19. $(5, -1)$ $(5, -6)$ _____

20. $(2, 2)$ $(7, 2)$ _____

21. $(3, 1)$ $(-1, 2)$ _____

7-5

Find the slope and y-intercept of each line.

22. $3x - 2y = 8$ _____

23. $5y - 15 = x$ _____

7-8

Determine whether the graphs of the equations are parallel.

24. $y - 2 = -2x$
$3y - 2 = -6x$ _____

25. $2y - 8 = 9x$
$3y - 7 = 4x$ _____

MIXED REVIEW 15

For use after Lesson 8-4

NAME _____

DATE _____

6-7   Factor.

1. $m^6 - 1$ _____

2. $3y^2 - 15y - 252$ _____

3. $2x^2 - 10x - 132$ _____

4. $11x^2 - 99$ _____

5. $xw - yw + xz - yz$ _____

6. $4a^2 - 4ac + c^2$ _____

5-4   Write in standard notation.

7. 1.75×10^5 _____

8. 3.14×10^{-3} _____

7-4   Find the slopes, if they exist, of the lines containing these points.

9. $(-6, 4)$ $(42, 28)$ _____

10. $(0, -3)$ $(-5, 12)$ _____

Multiply.

5-10   **11.** $2y(3x^2y - 11)$ _____

12. $(3a^2 - 1)(2a + 3)$ _____

5-11   **13.** $(x^2 - 5x - 6)(3x + 4)$ _____

14. $(x^2 + 2x - 9)(2x^2 - 5x + 2)$ _____

7-6   Write an equation for each line that contains the given pair of points.

15. $(-4, -5)$ $(0, 3)$ _____

16. $(4, 1)$ $(-6, -4)$ _____

Solve.

3-10   **17.** What percent of 120 is 45? _____

18. Thirty-six is 20 percent of what number? _____

3-11   **19.** The sum of three consecutive integers is 72. Find the integers. _____

3-9   **20.** A car uses 14.4 gallons of gasoline to travel 360 miles. How many gallons would be required to drive 500 miles? _____

6-9   **21.** The product of two consecutive odd integers is 255. Find the integers. _____

8-2   **22.** The sum of two numbers is 45. Their difference is 71. Find the numbers. _____

8-4   **23.** The perimeter of a rectangle is 39.2 cm. The length is 3.4 cm more than the width. Find the length and the width. _____

MIXED REVIEW 16
For use after Lesson 8-5

NAME _____

DATE _____

7-5   Graph each line using the *y*-intercept and slope.

    1. $3x + 3y = 15$

    2. $x = 2$

    3. $y = 2x + 4$

    4. $y = -1$

    5. $y = 3x - 2$

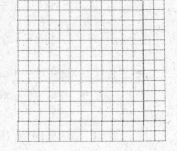

6-1   Find five factorizations for each monomial.

    6. $12a^2b$ _____   **7.** $50mn$ _____

6-2   Which of the following are differences of squares?

    8. $x^2 - 24a^2$ _____   **9.** $-16 + 49y^2$ _____   **10.** $121m^4 - n^2$ _____

6-3   Which of the following are trinomial squares?

    11. $a^2 - 8a + 16$ _____   **12.** $3x^2 + 6x + 1$ _____   **13.** $y^2 + 4y + 3$ _____

5-8   Give the additive inverse.

    14. $3a^2 - 6a + 10$ _____   **15.** $x^4 - 9y^2$ _____

7-6   Write an equation in slope-intercept form.

    16. The line with slope $= -1$, *y*-intercept $= (0, 4)$ _____

    17. The line that contains $(3, 3)$ and $(-9, -5)$ _____

    Solve.

8-3   **18.** $0.2x + 0.3y = 0.1$ **19.** $5m + \;\;n = 8$
              $0.3x - 0.1y = 0.7$ _____ $3m - 4n = 14$ _____

6-8   **20.** Find the number whose square is 15 more than twice the number. _____

8-5   **21.** It took a boat 5 hours to travel upstream and back.
           The current was 3 mi/h and the return trip took
           1 hour. Find the speed of the boat in still water. _____

MIXED REVIEW 17

For use after Lesson 9-2

NAME _____

DATE _____

7-8 ___ Determine whether the graphs of the equations are parallel, perpendicular, or neither.

1. $y = 3 + 5x$
$3x - y = -2$ _____

2. $-3x + 6y = 2$
$y = -2x - 10$ _____

3. $x + 6 = y$
$y - x = -2$ _____

5-3 ___ Simplify.

4. $\dfrac{-12a^2bc^4}{-3abc^2}$ _____

5. $\dfrac{m^6}{m^4}$ _____

6. $\dfrac{9x^3y}{3x}$ _____

7. $\dfrac{t^3}{t^3}$ _____

5-4 ___ Write using scientific notation.

8. 0.00381 _____

9. 17.662 _____

10. 36,840,000 _____

6-7 ___ Factor.

11. $x^2 - 15x + 54$ _____

12. $8a^2 + 22a + 15$ _____

13. $m^3 - 2m^2 + 3m - 6$ _____

14. $18t^2 - 128$ _____

15. $3y^2 - 20y + 12$ _____

16. $x^2y^2 + 8xy + 12$ _____

3-7 ___ Solve for x.

17. $abx = c$ _____

18. $x - m = 15$ _____

19. $3a - 4x = 8$ _____

20. $4x + 5 = cx + 2$ _____

21. $ax - 3x = 5$ _____

22. $mx^2 = 5x$ _____

Solve.

8-2 ___ **23.** $5m + n = 8$
$3m - 4n = 14$ _____

24. $3b - a = -7$
$5a + 6b = 14$ _____

8-3 ___ **25.** $x + y = 9$
$2x - y = -3$ _____

26. $2x + y = 6$
$x - y = 3$ _____

27. The difference between two numbers is 11. Twice the smaller plus three times the larger number is 123. What are the numbers? _____

8-5 ___ **28.** A car leaves Sacramento for Los Angeles traveling 54 mi/hr. A half hour later another car leaves Sacramento for Los Angeles traveling 64 mi/hr. How long after the second car leaves will it pass the first car? _____

9-2 ___ **29.** $5 < 2x + 9 \leq 15$ _____

30. $-7 \leq 3x - 1 < 5$ _____

7-5   Find the slope and y-intercept of each line.

    1. $3x + 5y = 15$ _____   **2.** $1.2x + 0.6y = 1.8$ _____

    3. $12y = 8x - 16$ _____   **4.** $4x + 5y = 5$ _____

6-7   Factor.

    5. $15x^3 + 12x^2y^2$ _____   **6.** $x^2 - 6xy + 9y^2$ _____

    7. $x^2y^2 - 100$ _____   **8.** $5a^3 - 80ab^2$ _____

    9. $b^3 - b^2y - 5by + 5y^2$ _____   **10.** $40y^2 + 10y - 15$ _____

    11. $x^3 - 8x^2 + 16x$ _____   **12.** $4m^3 + 28m^2 + m + 7$ _____

6-8   Solve.

    13. $x^2 + 4x - 21$ _____   **14.** $x^2 + 18x + 81 = 0$ _____

    15. $5y^2 - 75y = 0$ _____   **16.** $x^2 + 5x = 8x + 40$ _____

8-2   Solve each system of equations.

    17. $\begin{aligned} x + y &= 9 \\ 2x - 5y &= -3 \end{aligned}$ _____   **18.** $\begin{aligned} -5y + 4x &= -9 \\ 15y + 3x &= -3 \end{aligned}$ _____

8-6   Translate to a system of equations and solve.

    19. A collection of nickels and dimes is worth \$16.05. There are 218 coins in all. How many are nickels and how many are dimes?

    20. Corrin is 23 years older than Beth. In 9 years, Corrin will be twice as old as Beth. How old are they now?

    _____

9-1   Write using roster notation.

    21. The set A of all positive multiples of 3 less than 25 _____

    22. The set B of all positive multiples of 4 less than 25 _____

    23. The set C of all integers that are perfect squares less than 25 _____

9-4   Solve and graph.

    24. $|2y - 4| < 6$ _____   **25.** $|x - 3| > 3$ _____

9-5   Determine whether the given point is a solution of the inequality $3x - 2y < 2$.

    26. $(0, 0)$ _____   **27.** $(-2, 3)$ _____

For use after Lesson 10-3

NAME _____

DATE _____

65

6-7 _____ Factor.

1. $3x^3 - 27x$ _____ **2.** $y^4 + 4y^2 + 4$ _____

3. $y^3 - y + 3y^2 - 3$ _____ **4.** $x^2 + 10xy + 25y^2$ _____

7-6 _____ Write an equation for the line that contains the given pair of points.

5. $(-3, 2)$ $(2, -6)$ _____ **6.** $(5, 2)$ $(-5, -4)$ _____

Solve and graph.

9-2 _____ **7.** $-3 < x - 1 < 4$ _____

9-4 _____ **8.** $|3 + a| > 2$ _____

9-2 _____ **9.** $x - 2 < -3$ or $x - 2 > 4$ _____

9-4 _____ **10.** $|3y| < 9$ _____

3-11 _____ **11.** If you add $\frac{2}{5}$ of a number to itself you get 63. What is the number? _____

4-5 _____ **12.** Todd would like to make five shelves of equal length from a single 16.5 ft board. What is the greatest length a shelf may be? _____

6-9 _____ **13.** The sum of the squares of two consecutive odd positive integers is 130. Find the integers. _____

5-4 _____ Write in standard notation.

14. 1.062×10^{-3} _____ **15.** 7.66×10^4 _____ **16.** 1.1101×10^2 _____

7-8 _____ Determine whether the graphs of the equations are parallel.

17. $2x = y - 3$
$6x - 27 = 3y$ _____

18. $2y = x + 1$
$4y - 2x + 24 = 0$ _____

19. $y + 3x = 1$
$2 - y = 3x$ _____

8-2 _____ Solve each system of equations.

20. $x - y = 10$
$3y = -2x$ _____

21. $8y + 4x = 42$
$8y - 3x = 21$ _____

10-3 _____ Divide and simplify.

22. $\dfrac{x^2 + 3x + 2}{2x} \div \dfrac{x^2 + 2x + 1}{x + 1}$ _____

23. $\dfrac{4x^2 - 16}{3x - 6} \div \dfrac{x^2 + 4x + 4}{3x}$ _____

MIXED REVIEW 20

For use after Lesson 10-5

NAME _____

DATE _____

10-2   Multiply or divide and simplify.

1. $\dfrac{2x + 2}{x - 3} \cdot \dfrac{x^2 - 9}{x^2 - 1}$ _____

2. $\dfrac{12m}{m^2 - 9} \cdot \dfrac{m(m + 3)}{3m}$ _____

3. $\dfrac{a + c}{3a} \div \dfrac{a + c}{10a}$ _____

4. $\dfrac{5x - 15}{x - 2} \div \dfrac{7(x - 3)}{x^2 - 4}$ _____

5-4   Write using scientific notation.

5. 0.005113 _____

6. 683,054 _____

Solve.

8-6   **7.** A collection of nickels and quarters is worth $18.50. There are 118 coins in all. How many are nickels and how many are quarters?

_____

8-4   **8.** The perimeter of a rectangular garden is 94 m. The length is 13 m more than the width. Find the length and the width.

_____

7-5   Find the slope and the y-intercept of each line.

9. $6x + 2y = 10$ _____

10. $4x = y - 9$ _____

11. $3y - 1 = 11 + 9x$ _____

9-6   Solve these systems by graphing.

12. $y \le x$
$x > 2$

13. $x + y < 2$
$x \ge y$

14. $x - y > 1$
$y > 2$

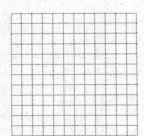

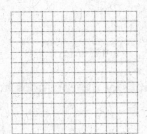

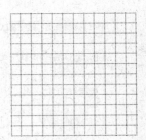

5-3   Simplify.

15. $\dfrac{9x^6}{6x^4}$ _____

16. $\dfrac{24x^4y}{-8xy}$ _____

17. $\dfrac{ab^{10}c^4}{3abc^3}$ _____

18. $\dfrac{a^2 - 9}{a^2 - 4a + 3}$ _____

19. $\dfrac{a^2 + 3a - 10}{a^2 - 9a + 14}$ _____

20. $\dfrac{2a^3 - 6a^2 - 8a}{4a^2 - 16a}$ _____

10-5   Find the least common multiple (LCM).

21. $x + 5, x^2 - 25$ _____

22. $3m - 21, m^2 - 49$ _____

23. $a + b, a - b$ _____

66

MIXED REVIEW 21

For use after Lesson 11-1

NAME _____

DATE _____

Add or subtract.

5-7 **1.** $(3x^2 - 9x + 5) - (8x + 11)$ _____ **2.** $(a^2 + 6ab - b^2) + (10 - a^2 + 3ab)$ _____

5-8 **3.** $(3x^2 - 5xy + y^2) - (11 - 6xy)$ _____ **4.** $(m^3 - 6m^2 + 6) - (m^2 - 9 + 3m^3)$ _____

10-4 **5.** $\dfrac{x^2 - 9}{x + 1} - \dfrac{3x^2 + 5}{x + 1}$ _____ **6.** $\dfrac{a + 3}{a + 1} + \dfrac{3a}{a + 1}$ _____

10-5 **7.** $\dfrac{5a}{a + 1} + \dfrac{2}{3a + 3}$ _____ **8.** $\dfrac{6}{a^2 - 4} + \dfrac{a}{a + 2}$ _____

9. $\dfrac{5y + 3}{2y} - \dfrac{2y + 1}{y}$ _____ **10.** $\dfrac{y - 1}{y - 4} - \dfrac{4}{y^2 - 16}$ _____

6-7 Factor.

11. $-8x^2 + 16x + 120$ _____ **12.** $18 - 2x^2$ _____

13. $2y^2 - 15y - 27$ _____ **14.** $9a^2 - 30a + 25$ _____

15. $3m^3 - 3m^2 - 6m$ _____ **16.** $-x^2 + 12x - 36$ _____

17. $25t^2 + 10t + 1$ _____ **18.** $x^4 - x^2y - 2y^2$ _____

7-6 Write an equation for the line that contains the given pair of points.

19. $(5, -2)$ $(-10, 7)$ _____ **20.** $(4, 3)$ $(-1, -7)$ _____

7-8 Determine whether the graphs of the equations are parallel.

21. $2y = 6x + 2$
$28 + 4y = 12x$ _____ **22.** $4y + 1 = 3x$
$3y - 2 = 4x$ _____

Solve.

9-3 **23.** $|2x - 5| = 3$ _____ **24.** $|x - 9| = -1$ _____

25. $|2y| \leq 5$ _____ **26.** $|-3a + 5| > 10$ _____

10-6 **27.** $5 = \dfrac{2x + 6}{4} + \dfrac{x - 2}{3}$ _____ **28.** $\dfrac{8x + 3}{9} + \dfrac{5x - 7}{4} = \dfrac{19x + 3}{12}$ _____

6-8 **29.** $2x^2 - 32 = 0$ _____ **30.** $x^2 + 21 = 10x$ _____

31. $y(3y - 9) = 0$ _____ **32.** $x^2 + 25 = 10x$ _____

11-1 Identify each square root as rational or irrational.

33. $\sqrt{100}$ _____ **34.** $\sqrt{1000}$ _____ **35.** $\sqrt{99}$ _____ **36.** $-\sqrt{4}$ _____

Multiply or divide.

5-10 **1.** $(2x + 7)(2x - 7)$ _____   **2.** $(a + 5)(a^2 - 2)$ _____

3. $(3m - 5)^2$ _____   **4.** $(2t + 9)^2$ _____

5-11 **5.** $(a^2 - 2a + 1)(2a + 3)$ _____   **6.** $(2m^2 - 11m + 6)(m - 5)$ _____

10-3 **7.** $\dfrac{y - 3}{y^2 - 9} \div \dfrac{4}{y + 3}$ _____   **8.** $\dfrac{x + 2}{x - 5} \div \dfrac{x + 2}{x - 1}$ _____

9. $\dfrac{c^2 - 9}{a^2 + a} \div \dfrac{c + 3}{a + 1}$ _____   **10.** $\dfrac{m^2 - n^2}{m^2 n^2} \div \dfrac{5m + 5n}{mn}$ _____

10-2 **11.** $\dfrac{6x^2}{x + 1} \cdot \dfrac{x^2 - 1}{3x^2}$ _____   **12.** $\dfrac{6y^3}{x^2} \cdot \dfrac{3x^2}{y^2}$ _____

11-4 **13.** $\sqrt{6m^3}\,\sqrt{2m}$ _____   **14.** $\sqrt{2}\,\sqrt{7x}$ _____   **15.** $\sqrt{xy}\,\sqrt{yz}\,\sqrt{xz}$ _____

11-5 **16.** $\dfrac{\sqrt{15}}{\sqrt{5}}$ _____   **17.** $\dfrac{\sqrt{50x^3}}{\sqrt{10x}}$ _____   **18.** $\sqrt{\dfrac{72}{40}}$ _____

Translate to an equation and solve.

3-10 **19.** Money is invested in a savings account at 8% simple
interest. After one year there is $513 in the account.
How much was originally invested? _____

6-9 **20.** The square of a number is ten less than seven times
the number. Find the number. _____

8-6 **21.** A collection of quarters and dimes is worth $16.00.
There are 34 more dimes than quarters. How many of
each are there? _____

10-5 Find the least common multiple (LCM).

22. $y^2 - 25,\ 7y + 35$ _____   **23.** $12 - 4x,\ x^2 - 9$ _____

Simplify.

5-2 **24.** $(2m^5)^4$ _____   **25.** $(-3a^7)^3$ _____   **26.** $(5xy^2)^2$ _____

10-1 **27.** $\dfrac{4a^2 - 9b^2}{2a + 3b}$ _____   **28.** $\dfrac{3 - m}{4(m - 3)}$ _____   **29.** $\dfrac{3y - 12}{3y + 9}$ _____

11-2 **30.** $\sqrt{49a^2}$ _____   **31.** $\sqrt{(x + 2)^2}$ _____   **32.** $\sqrt{m^2 n^2}$ _____

11-5 **33.** $\dfrac{\sqrt{100}}{\sqrt{25}}$ _____   **34.** $\sqrt{\dfrac{45}{25}}$ _____   **35.** $\dfrac{\sqrt{448}}{\sqrt{7}}$ _____

6-2 Which of the following are differences of two squares?

1. $10x^2 - 100$ _____ 2. $9x^2 + 81$ _____ 3. $16x^2 - 25$ _____

4. $a^2b^2 - a^2c^2$ _____ 5. $49 - x^2$ _____ 6. $121y^2 - 80$ _____

7-6 Write an equation for each line that contains the given pair of points.

7. $(-3, -2)$ $(2, 13)$ _____ 8. $(-8, -3)$ $(4, 2)$ _____

10-5 Find the least common multiple (LCM).

9. $5m + 15, m^2 - 9$ _____ 10. $y - 3, 9 - 3y$ _____ 11. $a^2 - 25, a + 5$ _____

11-5 Rationalize the denominator.

12. $\dfrac{\sqrt{6}}{\sqrt{5}}$ _____ 13. $\dfrac{\sqrt{10}}{\sqrt{3}}$ _____ 14. $\dfrac{\sqrt{27}}{\sqrt{3}}$ _____ 15. $\dfrac{\sqrt{2}}{\sqrt{7}}$ _____

16. $\sqrt{\dfrac{x}{3}}$ _____ 17. $\sqrt{\dfrac{5}{y}}$ _____ 18. $\dfrac{\sqrt{24c^3}}{\sqrt{6}}$ _____ 19. $\dfrac{\sqrt{18y}}{\sqrt{2}}$ _____

Factor.

6-7 20. $7a^2 - 14a + 49$ _____ 21. $m^2 - 5m - 36$ _____

22. $-3x^2 - 3x + 18$ _____ 23. $x^3 + 3x^2 - 10x$ _____

11-3 24. $-\sqrt{72}$ _____ 25. $\sqrt{25y^2}$ _____

26. $\sqrt{81m}$ _____ 27. $\sqrt{x^2 - 10x + 25}$ _____

5-4 Write using scientific notation.

28. $17{,}430$ _____ 29. 0.0301 _____ 30. 0.000009726 _____

Multiply and collect like terms.

5-9 31. $(3x - 7)(5x + 2)$ _____ 32. $(3m^2 + 2)(m^2 + 6)$ _____

5-11 33. $(x^2 - 6x + 9)(x - 2)$ _____ 34. $(5y^2 - 4)(2y^2 + 11y - 1)$ _____

11-4 35. $\sqrt{xy}\sqrt{yz}$ _____ 36. $\sqrt{2a}\sqrt{8a}$ _____ 37. $\sqrt{3y^3}\sqrt{8y^4}$ _____

12-1 Find the indicated outputs for these functions.

38. $f(t) = t^3 + t + 1$; find $f(0), f(-2), f(2)$ _____

39. $f(b) = b^2 + b - 2$; find $f(-1), f(1), f(-4)$ _____

9-1

Writing using roster notation/

1. The set A of all integers that are perfect squares between 20 and 100 _____

2. The set B of all positive integer factors of 36 _____

3. The set of C of all integers that are multiples of 5 between —18 and 23 _____

Divide.

10-3

4. $\dfrac{5y-5}{2} \div \dfrac{y-1}{8y}$ _____

5. $\dfrac{mn+n^2}{m} \div \dfrac{m^2-n^2}{mn^2}$ _____

10-9

6. $\left(x^2 - 7x + 3\right) \div (x-2)$ _____

7. $\left(4y^2 + 18y - 9\right) \div (2y+1)$ _____

11-5

8. $\dfrac{\sqrt{75}}{\sqrt{3}}$ _____

9. $\dfrac{\sqrt{36y}}{\sqrt{9}}$ _____

10. $\dfrac{\sqrt{99c}}{\sqrt{11}}$ _____

11. $\dfrac{\sqrt{56y^3}}{\sqrt{7}}$ _____

11-7

Use the Pythagorean theorem to find the hypotenuse (c) of the legs $(a$ and $b)$ of a right triangle.

12. $c = 15, \ a = 9, \ b =$ _____

13. $a = 5, \ b = 12, \ c =$ _____

14. $a = \sqrt{5}, \ c = \sqrt{11}, \ b =$ _____

15. $b = 7, \ c = 7\sqrt{2}, \ a =$ _____

5-4

Write using standard notation.

16. 1.6038×10^{-4} _____

17. 7.623×10^6 _____

Solve.

8-3

18. The sum of two numbers is 32. One half the first number plus one third of the second number is 14. Find the numbers

_____

10-8

19. Nut mix A is 40% peanuts and nut mix B is 65% peanuts. How much of each is needed to make 40 lb of a mix that is 55% peanuts?

_____

11-2

Determine the replacements for x that make the expression a real number.

20. $\sqrt{x-7}$ _____

21. $\sqrt{x^2+1}$ _____

22. $\sqrt{2x}$ _____

23. $\sqrt{x^2-2}$ _____

12-3

Write a linear function and solve.

24. Jerome earned $4.00 an hour for cleaning an attic, plus a bonus of $5.00 He worked for 5 hours. How much did he earn?

_____

25. Twyle bought 5 yards of ribbon for $2.50 a yard, plus there was a flat service charge of $2.00. What was the total cost of the ribbon?

_____

5-8   Find the additive inverse.

1. $2x^2 - 5x + 6$ _____   **2.** $-3x^3 + 5$ _____   **3.** $x^5 - 9x^2 - 1$ _____

Solve.

9-4   **4.** $|4m| < 12$ _____   **5.** $|3 + y| > 2$ _____

10-6   **6.** $x - \dfrac{5}{x} = 4$ _____   **7.** $\dfrac{3}{4x} - \dfrac{2}{x + 5} = 0$ _____

11-9   **8.** $\sqrt{x^2 + 9} - 5 = 0$ _____   **9.** $\sqrt{x + 5} - 3 = 2$ _____

7-5   Find the slope of each line.

10. $3y = 5x - 1$ _____   **11.** $x - 7 = y + 2$ _____

8-1, 9-6   Solve by graphing.

12. $x - y = -2$
     $5y + 2 = x$

13. $y \geq x + 1$
     $2y > 1 - x$

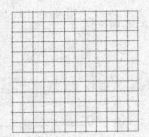 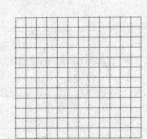

Simplify.

5-2   **14.** $(2m^2n^3)^3$ _____   **15.** $(-5x^2y^3)^2$ _____   **16.** $[(-x)^5]^2$ _____

10-3   **17.** $\dfrac{m + 3}{2m - 2} \div \dfrac{m^2 - 9}{m - 1}$ _____   **18.** $\dfrac{x^2 - 4x}{x + 1} \div \dfrac{x^2 - 16}{x^2 - 1}$ _____

Solve.

11-8   **19.** How long must a wire be to reach from the top of a
12-ft pole to a point on the ground 9 ft from the base? _____

6-9   **20.** Find the number whose square is 24 more than 5
times the number. _____

13-2   **21.** $x^2 = 7$ _____   **22.** $2x^2 = 8$ _____   **23.** $2x^2 = 8x$ _____

13-3

Complete the square.

1. $m^2 - 20m$ _____

2. $a^2 + 6a$ _____

3. $t^2 + 5t$ _____

4. $r^2 - 7r$ _____

5. $x^2 - 9x$ _____

6. $y^2 + 30y$ _____

6-7

Factor.

7. $-4x^2 + 8x + 64$ _____

8. $5m^2 - 60$ _____

9. $x^2 + 9x + 14$ _____

10. $3x^2 - 18x + 27$ _____

11. $x^3 + 2x^2 - x - 2$ _____

12. $10y^2 - 21y - 10$ _____

Solve by factoring. Complete the square if necessary.

6-8

13. $x^2 + 10 = 7x$ _____

14. $4y^2 = 25$ _____

15. $m^2 - 3m = 18$ _____

16. $4x^2 - 32x + 60 = 0$ _____

13-3

17. $x^2 + 2x - 4 = 0$ _____

18. $3x^2 + 2x - 5 = 0$ _____

19. $x^2 - 6x + 4 = 0$ _____

20. $x^2 + 8x - 6 = 0$ _____

13-4

Solve using the quadratic formula.

21. $8x^2 - 6x + 1 = 0$ _____

22. $x^2 - 5x - 6 = 0$ _____

23. $12x^2 + 7x + 1 = 0$ _____

24. $x^2 - 6x + 6 = 0$ _____

13-4

Find an equation of variation where y varies inversely as x. One pair of values is given.

25. $y = -2$ when $x = 5$ _____

26. $y = 0.3$ when $x = 2$ _____

7-6

Write an equation for the line that contains the given pair of points.

27. $(10, 0)$ $(-15, 10)$ _____

28. $(4, 9)$ $(-6, -16)$ _____

Solve.

6-9

29. The length of a rectangle is three times the width. The area is 867 cm². Find the length and the width.

_____

13-2

30. The sum of $2000 is invested at interest rate r, compounded annually. In two years it grows to $2880. What is the interest rate?

_____

13-5

Solve each rational equation.

31. $x + \dfrac{2}{x} = -3$ _____

32. $\dfrac{1}{16} - \dfrac{1}{x^2} = 0$ _____